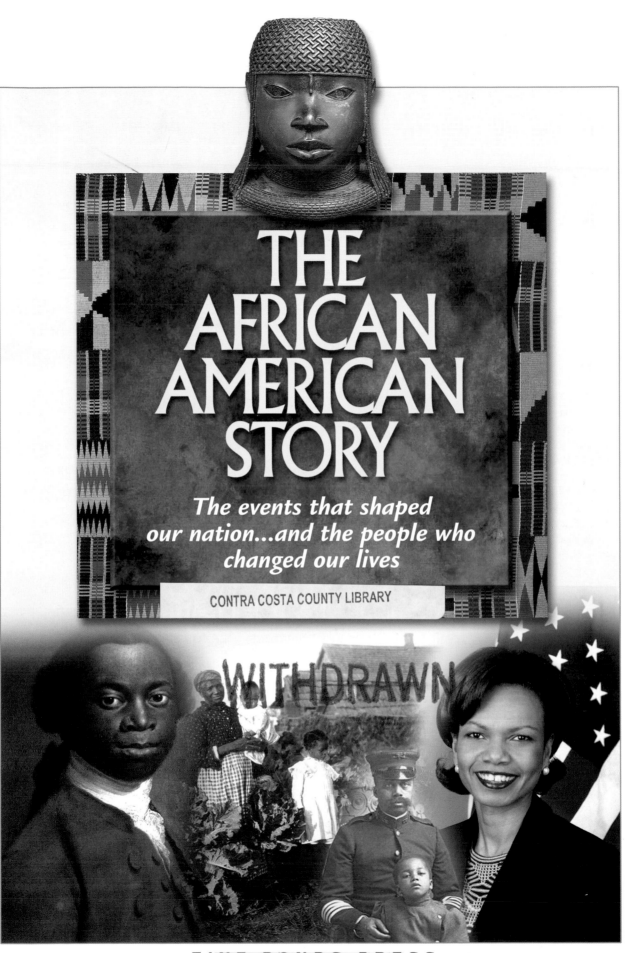

THE AFRICAN AMERICAN STORY

The events that shaped our nation...and the people who changed our lives

FIVE PONDS PRESS
WACCABUC, NEW YORK

The author gratefully acknowledges the enormous contributions and guidance of:

Dr. Lillian S. Williams, Chair & Associate Professor of African American Studies, State University of New York, Buffalo

Dr. Brenda Stevenson, Chair, Interdepartmental Program in Afro-American Studies, UCLA

Dr. Jose C. Moya, Professor of History, UCLA and Barnard College

Dr. Virginia Yans-McLaughlin, Board of Governors Distinguished Service Professor of American History, Rutgers University

FIVE PONDS PRESS ADVISORY GROUP:

Dr. Melissa Matusevich, Asst. Professor, Curriculum & Instruction, East Carolina University

Dr. Donald Zeigler, Professor of Geography and Political Science, Old Dominion University

REVIEWERS: Special thanks for the encouragment and contributions of the following educators:

Hassan Adeeb, Social Studies Learning Charts

Jason Deryck-Mahlke, John Jay H.S. (NY)

Bree Linton, Henrico County (VA)

Kathy Morrison, Retired Supervisor for Social Studies, K-12, Hanover County, (VA)

Susan Orr, Fairfax County (VA)

Anita Parker, Virginia Beach (VA)

Brenda Randolph, Africa Access

Lara Samuels, Hanover County (VA)

Denise Williams, Virginia Beach (VA)

Five Ponds Press books are available at a special discount when purchased in bulk for educational use. Contact Special Sales Dept. at Five Ponds Press or email info@fivepondspress.com

Copyright ©2007, by Joy Masoff. All rights reserved.
Published by Five Ponds Press, Waccabuc, NY 10597
Library of Congress Cataloging-in-Publication data available
ISBN 13: 978-0-9727156-9-0   ISBN 10: 0-9727156-9-X
First printing January 2007
10 9 8 7 6 5 4 3 2 1   Printed in Peru

THE AFRICAN AMERICAN STORY
TABLE OF CONTENTS

WITH HEADS HELD HIGH

"It is not what you are called, but what you answer to."

OLD AFRICAN PROVERB

Look at these faces. Some are famous, others are not, but they all tell an amazing story—a tale of love and loss, triumph and tears, faith and dignity.

These are the faces of joy and sorrow, the faces of grit and strength, the faces of people whose ancestors were taken from their homelands and forced against their will into a life they did not want.

These eyes have seen cruelty and kindness. These ears have heard lovely stories and beautiful music. These mouths have sung sweet songs and given powerful speeches. These arms have held babies, hit home runs, soared in space, and saved lives.

A STORY OF TRIUMPH

How did millions of people from Africa come to live in America? Why were they treated so badly for so many years? How did they survive and fight their way to freedom?

This story begins more than 500 years ago on the other side of the world—in a very different time and place. The world stood on the edge of sweeping change as people began to leave their little towns and villages behind to sail across vast oceans to strange new lands. Let the journey begin…

JACKIE ROBINSON

MAE JEMISON

IN AFRICA

"Unless you know the road you have come down, you cannot know where you are going"

**TEMNE PROVERB
—SIERRA LEONE**

A mask pendant worn by the Oba (king) of Benin in the 1500s.

EUROPE

ASIA

AFRICA
As seen from space

MOROCCO

EGYPT
Nile River

NUBIA

Sahara Desert

SONGHAI
MALI

AKSUM

BENIN

Atlantic Ocean

Indian Ocean

Before you can begin to understand how Africans came to live in America, you must first learn about the amazing land they left behind.

ARE WE ALL AFRICANS?

Many scientists believe that Africa, our planet's second largest **continent,** was the place where human life began—the starting point as our forebearers began to fan out across the globe about 70,000 years ago. Africa had rich forests and lush grasslands that were perfect for grazing animals. Beneath the soil lay gold, silver, precious gems, and salt—some of the most valuable things on Earth.

Ahmose Nefertari was a powerful Egyptian ruler about 3500 years ago.

MOTHER OF CIVILIZATIONS

More than 5,000 years ago, some of the world's first great **civilizations** rose up along the Nile River. In Egypt, rulers built huge pyramids and grand temples. Farther south along the Nile lay Aksum and Nubia, whose great achievements include building even more pyramids than the Egyptians! Nubian kings ruled Egypt for a century. In the West the vast empires of Ghana, Mali, and Songhai grew rich and powerful. In Nigeria a 745-mile long wall snaked through the great city of Benin. The African continent was indeed a birthplace of modern civilization.

A painting of the ruins of an ancient Nubian palace.

One of the many amazing mosques—places of prayer—in the African country of Mali, a great center of learning in the 1300s and 1400s.

WHERE THE WORLD MET

By 1300 over 1,000 different languages were spoken in Africa. There were hundreds of ethnic groups, each with its own special customs—some as different from one another as the Irish are from the Japanese. There were large universities where Europeans came to study medicine and early forms of surgery. There were libraries filled with books. Farmers grew rice and millet (a type of grain). They raised herds of cattle and goats. Artists wove beautiful textiles and created stunning sculptures. Storytellers and musicians made imaginations soar with tales of heroic deeds.

Trading was an important part of life, especially in West Africa, and the great marketplaces of Mali became a crossroad of the world. Merchants flocked there bringing silks, jewels, and horses. There was very little crime, and the cities were safe at a time when much of Europe was a dangerous place to live. The traders returned home with gold, ivory, precious metals, and salt. They also sometimes brought another cargo back with them—men and women who had been captured in battle—**slaves**.

Mansa Musa, a king of Mali in the 1300s, was one of the wealthiest men on Earth.

Words to know

▶ **Continent**—
(<u>con</u>-tin-ent)
A large land mass.

▶ **Civilizations**—
(siv-uh-luh-<u>zay</u>-shuns)
Groups of people living together who have developed art, music, science, and rules to live by.

▶ **Slaves**—
People who are bought and sold and who work without pay. They have little say in their lives.

500 C.E.* -1076	1230–1450	1400s	1450	1500s
KINGDOM OF GHANA RISES IN WEST AFRICA AS THE DARK AGES GRIP EUROPE.	MALI BECOMES A CENTER OF WORLD TRADE AND LEARNING.	SAILORS FROM PORTUGAL BEGIN EXPLORING WEST AFRICA'S COAST.	CIVIL WARS IN MALI. SONGHAI KINGS TAKE CONTROL.	THE TRANS-ATLANTIC SLAVE TRADE BEGINS.

*Historians today use C.E. ("Common Era") instead of A.D. ("Anno Domino") to mark the start of the modern calendar.

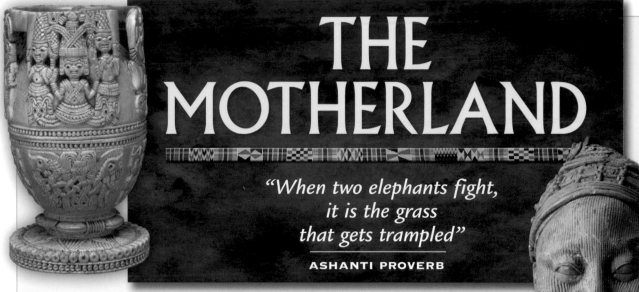

THE MOTHERLAND

"When two elephants fight, it is the grass that gets trampled"

ASHANTI PROVERB

This Yoruba vase from the 1500s was carved from an elephant tusk.

Words to know

▶ **Caravan–**
(<u>cah</u>-ruh-van)
A long line of travelers, often traders, traveling with camels.

Slavery has been around for thousands of years all over the world. People on every continent owned slaves. In fact, the word "slave" comes from "Slavs"—the people of Eastern Europe. In ancient Rome there were so many Slavic people serving as unpaid workers that the name stuck.

When wars were fought, captured soldiers became slaves. When towns were conquered, the villagers became slaves. Sometimes people were sentenced to a life of slavery instead of jail because of crime or debt. Africa was no different.

DESERT CROSSINGS

Many slave traders grew quite rich. Arab slave traders from East Africa met traders from West Africa in the center of the African continent to buy and sell people. Traders bought Africans in small numbers and moved them north along the *trans-Saharan trade routes* in long **caravans**. The Sahara is a huge desert about the size of the mainland United States, and it took weeks to cross, but all that was about to change in the 1400s.

The ruins of a once-busy city on the trans-Saharan trade route in Morocco, a country in North Africa.

A modern day caravan crosses the Sahara.

Caravels were sturdy sailing ships—good in the rough seas of the Atlantic Ocean.

EUROPE

ASIA

AFRICA
Sahara Desert

*TRANS-SAHARAN
SLAVE TRADE TO
NORTH AFRICA*

*TRANS-SAHARAN
SLAVE TRADE
TO ASIA*

Atlantic Ocean

*TRANS-ATLANTIC
SLAVE TRADE
TO THE AMERICAS*

Indian Ocean

1
2
3
4
5
6
7

A CHANGING WORLD

About 600 years ago ships from Europe began to sail south along Africa's west coast as sailors from Portugal tried to find trading routes around the tip of Africa to India. It was much faster to travel by sea than it was to cross the Sahara by camel, so the trading cities that lay along the caravan routes had fewer traders stopping by. Life became difficult as business declined. Fighting broke out between rival groups or **clans,** and once-safe places became dangerous. The Europeans had something deadly to trade with—guns. With weapons, a king or clan leader was even more powerful!

REGIONS WHERE
MOST PEOPLE WERE
ENSLAVED IN THE
1700S

1. Senegal 2. Sierra Leone
3. Ghana 4. Mali
5. Nigeria 6. Congo and Angola
7. Mozambique

A FAMOUS YEAR

In 1493 Christopher Columbus brought big news back to Europe—tales of mysterious lands across the sea that soon became known as the Americas. Before his trans-Atlantic trip, Columbus was a navigator on European ships sailing along the coast of West Africa. Some historians think that West Africans had been sailing to the Americas for centuries before Columbus did. Perhaps their tales inspired his trip.

By the early 1500s, the fate of Africa's people had become tied to the lands on the other side of the ocean. For the people who lived near the coasts of the African continent—especially the Mende, the Yoruba, the Ibo and others—life was about to take a terrible turn. At first by the hundreds, then in rapidly growing numbers, they were torn from their motherland and dragged to a strange new world.

Words to know

▶ **Clans–**
Groups of people related by blood or marriage.

Hundreds of years before Columbus, African sailors may have crossed the Atlantic in ships like these modern-day boats, called dhows.

9

ACROSS AN OCEAN

"... there was nothing heard but the rattling of chains, smacking of whips, and the groans and cries of our fellow men."

OTTOBAH CUGOANO—
KIDNAPPED AS A CHILD IN GHANA

How would you feel if someone grabbed you and took you from your home—*forever*? Imagine being forced to march for days with strange people yelling at you and hitting you. That is what happened in parts of Africa beginning in the 1500s. Some people were captured as prisoners of war. Others were used like money to repay debts, but why was there such a big demand for slaves in the first place?

WHEN THREE WORLDS MET

The Americas were rich with valuable resources such as gold, silver, lumber, and furs. The Europeans wanted all these riches, but they needed workers to gather these things. Why not put the American Indians to work?

Something awful happened when the Europeans first came to the Americas. They did not know it, but they carried diseases to which the first Americans had never been exposed. The Indians became sick, and many millions died. The survivors could not be forced to work and simply ran into the woods or vanished inland. *Now* who was going to do all the work?

The Europeans tried using convicts, but there were still not enough workers. Some people came as **indentured servants** whose trips were paid for by wealthy businessmen, but as word got out that life was dangerous in the new colonies, few folks were willing to risk dying for a job, so the Europeans looked to another continent for skilled workers—Africa!

Words to know

▶ **Indentured Servants–**
People who worked for a set period of time— usually from three to five years—in exchange for a trip to the New World, clothing, money, farm equipment, and some training. Many died before getting what was owed to them.

NORTH
AMERICA

Atlantic Ocean

EUROPE

SOUTHERN
COLONIES

3

1

AFRICA

WEST INDIES

2

Most enslaved Africans were taken
to Brazil and the Caribbean.

2

ELMINA

SOUTH
AMERICA

BRAZIL

2

THE TRIANGLE OF TRADE

**1. Manufactured goods such as guns and rum were
loaded aboard ships in Europe and brought to Africa.**

**2. In the MIDDLE PASSAGE, humans replaced the
crates and barrels on the trip from Africa to America.**

**3. Loaded with raw materials including lumber, sugar,
and cotton, ships left the Americas for Europe.**

KIDNAPPED!

Elmina in Ghana was
the biggest and best
known of the slave
forts. About 30,000
terrified prisoners a
year passed through
the narrow "Door of
no Return."

How could the Europeans get Africans to come
to America? At first, they bought those who were
already enslaved—mostly prisoners of war. As
their desire for black workers grew, they hired
people to kidnap Africans, imprison them, then
send them to be slaves in America. Many of the captured
Africans did not become as ill as the Indians had from European diseases because
they had learned to prevent and treat smallpox and other illnessess. The new diseases
of the Americas did not affect them as much as they did European
workers, so slave traders began buying more and more Africans.

FORTS OF FEAR

The prisoners were taken to giant slave forts owned by European
nations on the west coast of Africa, where they were held for months
until they could be shipped to the Americas. To keep captives from
escaping, slave traders separated people who spoke the same languages
so they could not plot revolts. In the meantime, as the demand for
more slaves grew, wars broke out between African nations. Innocent
people were kidnapped as they went about their everyday lives.
Between 1500 and 1880, more than ten million Africans were chained
together, packed aboard filthy boats, and sent to the Americas.

The Door of
No Return at
Elmina was
tiny to prevent
escape.

11

What awaited the captured Africans after they left the slave forts? What happened on the long journey across the Atlantic Ocean?

DEATH AT SEA

The trip across the Atlantic Ocean was called the **Middle Passage** because it was the middle part of the triangle of trade. It was a nightmare. The captives were chained together and packed tightly below deck where they slept on wet, bare floors for weeks. They ate twice a day—a breakfast stew of beans, boiled yams, and scraps of foul meat, and a dinner mush of nasty-tasting oily horse beans. In good weather the Africans were allowed some fresh air on deck, simply to preserve their health. A dead slave was worthless.

THE MIDDLE PASSAGE

"I asked if we were to be eaten by these men with red faces and angry looks."

**OLAUDAH EQUIANO
AN ENSLAVED AFRICAN**

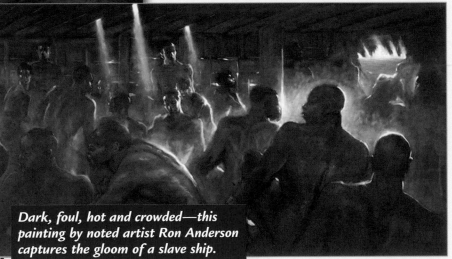

Dark, foul, hot and crowded—this painting by noted artist Ron Anderson captures the gloom of a slave ship.

Some English slaving captains liked to "tight-pack" their ships. They believed more slaves would mean higher profits. "Loose-packers" believed arriving with more people alive made better sense. This diagram showed captains how to use every square inch of a ship.

Sailors swung whips to make sure no one disobeyed, but many Africans fought back or jumped overboard, choosing death over the horrors at sea. Many more died from diseases caused by the lack of toilets and the filthy conditions. Others died of thirst. Some historians believe almost a quarter of the captives never made it to the Americas. For those who survived, life would never be the same.

A SAD WELCOME

When the boats finally docked in the Americas, the Africans were taken to slave yards. They were allowed to bathe and were given extra food to regain weight lost during the trip. On the day of the slave sales, they were rubbed all over with palm oil to hide the wounds and sores from the terrible journey across the sea.

I SAW HIM FIRST!

Plantation owners, or slave dealers, bought captives directly from the ship's captain. Slave dealers then held public auctions, where the enslaved were sold to the highest bidders. Some ships' captains held "scrambles," where buyers agreed to a price per person ahead of time. Then, on a signal, they would run in and grab the strongest, healthiest looking Africans they could get their hands on. Friendships formed at sea were ended. This was often the saddest moment of all.

NORTH AMERICA

SOUTH AMERICA

AFRICA

ATLANTIC SLAVE TRADE 1700-1810

6% went to North America

23% went to British West Indies

22% went to French West Indies

8% went to Dutch West Indies

10% went to Spanish America

31% went to Brazil

To be sold on board the Ship Bance-Island, on tuesday the 6th of May next, at Apley-Ferry; a choice cargo of about 250 fine healthy NEGROES, just arrived from the Windward & Rice Coast.—The utmost care has already been taken, and shall be continued, to keep them free from the least danger of being infected with the SMALL-POX, no boat having been on board, and all other communication with people from Charles-Town prevented. Austin, Laurens, & Appleby. N.B. Full one Half of the above Negroes have had the SMALL-POX in their own Country.

AN AMAZING LIFE

Olaudah Equiano

OLAUDAH EQUIANO wrote a famous book that told the story of his capture from an Ibo village when he was 10. He described his awful journey to the Caribbean and his move to Virginia. Eventually he was sold to a Quaker merchant in Philadelphia who let him buy his freedom in 1766.

Equiano's book caused a huge stir. He spent the rest of his life trying to end the slave trade. Some historians think he made up parts of his story to help free his people, but much of it was true.

For many years historians believed that the portrait shown at right was Olaudah Equiano. Today, some have begun to doubt that it is. Instead, they think this man may have been a servant in a London home.

IN A NEW LAND

*"No matter how far a stream flows,
It never forgets its source."*

YORUBA PROVERB—NIGERIA

England
France
Spain
Unclaimed
Russia
Holland
Portugal

EUROPE'S CLAIMS IN THE AMERICAS IN 1750

Some of the first Africans in the Americas came as sailors on Spanish ships in the late 1400s. In 1565 Africans helped build the first permanent European **colony** in what is now the United States—St. Augustine, Florida. Driven by a thirst for gold, Spaniards searched the Americas, while their diseases wiped out millions of natives. Soon these *"conquistadores"*—conquerors—found something almost as good as gold—sugar.

SO SWEET, SO BITTER

Most American colonies were all about profit. Back in Europe, companies owned by kings and queens or wealthy families paid to send settlers to work in the Americas. Huge sugar **plantations** soon covered islands such as Jamaica, Barbados, and Haiti. Finding gold in Brazil led to an even greater demand for workers. Africans—experienced farmers and miners—were the perfect labor force. Soon millions were being dragged across the ocean to America.

The first Africans to land in Virginia became indentured servants.

A NEW HARBOR

In 1619 a group of Africans aboard a Dutch ship landed in Jamestown, Virginia. These Africans had not been sold in the West Indies, so the ship's captain decided to try to unload them at a new English colony. It was to be the beginning of a terrible 400-year-long struggle for freedom.

ESTEBANICO *(about 1500-1539) was one of only four people to survive a Spanish expedition to the Americas. He spent eight years walking across the continent and was the first African to see what is now Texas, New Mexico, and Arizona.*

WHAT SAVED THE NEW COLONIES?

The First Crops

The warmer parts of the Americas were good places to raise crops that were in great demand in Europe, but each took a lot of work to grow, so the need for a large labor force grew. TOBACCO, a crop first grown by Native Americans, was prized. So was RICE, which was brought to the Americas by Africans. INDIGO, a plant from which a much-used blue dye was made, was also a big seller. In addition, SUGAR CANE, a major crop in the Caribbean, was also grown in Louisiana.

Enslaved Africans at work on a tobacco plantation in the early 1700s. Tobacco was a hard crop to grow. The leaves got buggy and had to be carefully hung to dry. The fields quickly lost their nutrients, so new areas always had to be prepared. It was a lot of work.

Slaves planting sugar cane on a Caribbean plantation.

Words to know

▶ **Colony–**
(col-uh-nee)
A group of people who settle far from home but keep close ties with their homeland.

▶ **Laws–**
Society's way of keeping order with rules we must follow.

▶ **Plantations–**
(plan-tay-shunz)
A very large farm on which one major cash crop is grown.

FAREWELL TO FREEDOM

The first Africans in Jamestown, and others in the years to come, were indentured servants. After a few years, they earned their freedom just like indentured Europeans, but there were never enough workers. *More* Africans were needed!

The Africans brought many skills with them. They knew a lot about farming and raising animals. Some were excellent sailors. They were weavers, craftspeople, miners, and experienced iron-workers. The sicknessess of the Americas did not kill them. The truth is, had it not been for all their hard work, the new colonies probably would not have survived.

At first the Africans had a chance to earn their freedom, but by 1640 the Virginia courts had sentenced at least one black servant to a life of slavery. Soon other **laws** were written that made children of enslaved mothers slaves as well. A slave had to work forever—not just a few years. A sad way of life was falling into place.

1607	1619	1640	1641	1663	1705
BRITISH START A NEW COLONY CALLED JAMESTOWN, VIRGINIA.	THE FIRST AFRICANS LANDED IN JAMESTOWN, VIRGINIA.	ROYAL AFRICAN COMPANY IS STARTED IN BRITAIN TO TRADE SLAVES.	MASSACHUSETTS BECOMES THE FIRST COLONY TO APPROVE SLAVERY.	A NEW VIRGINIA LAW DECLARES THAT ALL CHILDREN BORN TO SLAVE MOTHERS ARE SLAVES TOO.	VIRGINIA SLAVE CODES BECOME LAW, TAKING ALL RIGHTS AWAY FROM ENSLAVED PEOPLE.

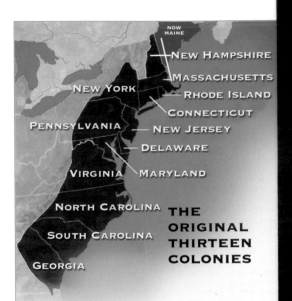

THE ORIGINAL THIRTEEN COLONIES

NEW HAMPSHIRE
MASSACHUSETTS
NEW YORK
RHODE ISLAND
CONNECTICUT
PENNSYLVANIA
NEW JERSEY
DELAWARE
VIRGINIA
MARYLAND
NORTH CAROLINA
SOUTH CAROLINA
GEORGIA
NOW MAINE

COLONIAL DAYS

"All servants imported and brought into the country...who were not Christians in their native country...shall be counted and be slaves."

VIRGINIA SLAVE LAW—1705

Between 1700 and 1800, more than ten million Africans came to North and South America. About half a million ended up on the mainland of North America, in the colonies controlled by Britain—the same colonies that would one day become the first "united" states.

The trans-Atlantic slave trade was now in full swing, with England (which had the world's biggest fleet) controlling most of it. Slavery was all about making money for the traders and slave owners—a *lot* of money.

NORTH OR SOUTH

In the early 1700s most enslaved Africans in the British colonies worked in the South. The need for farm workers in the North was not as great since the products in biggest demand in Europe—tobacco and cotton—would not grow there. In addition to field work, slaves served as sailors and craftspeople, maids and butlers, farm hands, cooks, nurses and nannies. Not all African Americans were enslaved in the early 1700s. Some were free, but all across the colonies a change was beginning to take place.

"I OWN YOU"

Most newcomers from Africa were either Muslims or prayed to the spirits of nature. New laws were passed that said that since the Africans were not Christians, they did not have any rights. Many could not get married or buy homes. Something important came to pass. The dark skin that protected Africans against the hot sun of their homeland now became proof that they "belonged" to someone else.

George Washington, America's great leader and first President, was a slave owner. This painting shows him with his overseer as his slaves take a water-break.

BORN INTO BONDAGE

Imagine waking up every day wondering if you will be taken from your family, beaten, or even killed. That was the fate of many African Americans as slavery took hold in America. It was a terrible way to live, yet somehow they managed to hold on to hope. Some escaped and joined up with American Indians. Others quietly fought back in small ways, secretly breaking their tools, working slowly, or pretending to be sick. Some took more extreme measures, getting other slaves to join them in escaping and sometimes even killing those who tried to stop them. They usually were killed as they tried to flee.

SEEDS OF REVOLT

In 1676 former indentured servants, both African and European, were living side by side in a few colonies, and the amount of money a person had mattered more than skin color when it came to being friends or taking sides. One day, after a fight between a white planter named Nathanial Bacon and Virginia's governor over Indian land rights, Bacon's black *and* white neighbors got together to push the governor out. ***Bacon's Rebellion*** was one of the first times blacks raised weapons against the government, and it scared many slave owners. "What will keep armed blacks from using guns to free their fellow Africans?" they thought. Bacon's fight meant the end of the indenture system. However, slavery soon became the most important form of labor in the southern colonies.

Still, African Americans clung to their roots. They left lasting marks on the new colonies. The ways Americans spoke, farmed, ate, built homes, danced, raised families, prayed, practiced medicine, and played music were all being influenced by the spirit and soul of Africa.

A MAJOR MILESTONE

The Great Awakenings

1738-1776

Christianity became a big part of African American lives in the mid-1700s as blacks were "awakened" to Jesus' teachings. Preachers such as RICHARD ALLEN traveled all over, sharing Bible stories and starting black churches. Many slaves learned to read by reading the Bible; they found comfort in the promise that "the meek shall inherit the Earth."

Richard Allen 1760-1831

LIBERTY OR DEATH!

"I do hereby declare all indented servants, negroes, or others, free, that are able to bear arms..."

**LORD DUNMORE, GOVERNOR OF VIRGINIA
1775**

What did the colonies look like in 1770? They were growing wealthier every day, shipping raw materials—lumber, furs, and especially tobacco—to Europe. Port cities like New York and Boston were filled with ships. There were almost half a million African Americans in the colonies hard at work, day-in and day-out.

About this time, some white colonists began to feel they were being treated unfairly by their mother country, Great Britain. Their taxes were too high, and they had little say in their government, but the more the colonists complained, the more troops came from Britain to police them. The colonists began to talk about breaking away from Britain. They spoke about freedom and liberty. Things were tense, and some colonists—both black and white—were getting angrier and angrier.

Peter Salem, a hero at the Battle of Bunker Hill, readies his musket.

BOSTON'S MASSACRE

One cold March night in 1770, a small, rowdy group of colonists started throwing hunks of ice and rocks at an armed British guard in Boston. More soldiers appeared, and shots were fired. When the smoke cleared, a former slave, Crispus Attucks, lay dead in the snow, the first to die for America's freedom. His death, along with the others slain that night, helped push the colonies into a **War of Independence** from Britain.

Full-blown battles in Massachusetts followed soon after at Concord, Lexington, and Bunker Hill with black heroes such as Salem Poor, Peter Salem, and Prince Hall at the front lines. But as George Washington took command of the **Continental Army** in 1775, he told every black soldier to go home. They were not welcome! As a slave owner, Washington knew that many people believed that black soldiers with guns in their hands could all too easily turn on the people who "owned them."

1775	1776	1777-78	1780	1781	1783	1787
THE FIRST SHOTS OF THE AMERICAN REVOLUTION ARE FIRED.	DECLARATION OF INDEPENDENCE WRITTEN. BATTLES CONTINUE.	WASHINGTON ALLOWS MEN OF COLOR TO JOIN THE ARMY.	MOST MAJOR BATTLES ARE BEING FOUGHT IN THE SOUTH.	BRITAIN SURRENDERS AT YORKTOWN, VIRGINIA.	LAST BRITISH FORCES LEAVE THE COLONIES.	THE CONSTITUTION, AN OFFICIAL SET OF LAWS, IS WRITTEN.

CHOOSING SIDES

In June 1772 an important law was passed in Britain that outlawed slavery there (slave *trading* however, still went on). By 1775 as war loomed, the British Governor of Virginia, Lord Dunsmore, asked enslaved African Americans to fight on Britain's side in exchange for freedom. Many blacks joined, hoping for a British victory. Faced with an all-out slave rebellion in the South as a result of Dunsmore's promise of freedom, Washington, too, asked blacks to join his army and promised them freedom as well.

ALL EQUAL?

In a stuffy hall in Philadelphia on a hot July day in 1776, one of the most important documents ever written was signed by America's leading citizens. Even though Thomas Jefferson was a slave owner, he and the other writers of the **Declaration of Independence** hoped to end slavery in the new United States. However, the Southerners who signed the Declaration had grown rich owning slaves, so the slave laws stayed.

America marched off to war. Things went poorly at first, and by the time George Washington and his troops limped off to Valley Forge in Pennsylvania in the winter of 1777, the army was a mess. Many soldiers had died while others simply quit. Washington had to recruit new soldiers, including blacks.

AT WAR'S END

Washington's new army proved to be brave fighters, and the war's tide turned—thanks, in part, to the new recruits. More than 5,000 African Americans earned their freedom fighting as Continental soldiers. And what about the blacks who fought for Britain? At the war's end 20,000 African American soldiers and their families left with the British and moved to Canada or to the African country of Sierra Leone. Sadly, some were reenslaved in the British Caribbean. A war had been fought to prove that "All men are created equal," but for most African Americans it still was not true.

MAJOR MILESTONES

Unsung Heroes

George Washington owed a lot to his African American troops. They taught him how to protect against deadly smallpox by scratching a drop of pox into soldiers' arms. Washington quickly learned that black soldiers fought bravely. Some people began to understand that if people of color were willing to die for their land, they deserved to live in freedom too. It was a beginning...

A young black soldier saves the life of George Washington's cousin at South Carolina's Battle of Cowpens in 1781.

19

After the War of Independence ended, the new nation began to take shape, but it needed rules to organize the country. The writers of the **Constitution of the United States** (which became law in 1789), had a problem. There were wealthy, powerful people in the South who felt slavery was okay. Most folks in the North did not. In order to get the Constitution approved, it became necessary to **compromise**—to let pro-slavery people have their say. As a result, the Constitution made slaves "three-fifths" of a person on state tax rolls and said that slaves caught escaping, even to a state with no slavery, would be swiftly returned to their owners.

NORTH

"Some view our sable [brown] race with scornful eye."

PHYLLIS WHEATLEY • 1773

Learn more about Benjamin Banneker on page 68

Words to know

▶ **Constitution–**
(con-sti-<u>too</u>-shun)
The basic laws of a nation.

▶ **Compromise–**
(<u>com</u>-pro-mize)
A middle ground between two extremes.

▶ **Emancipation–**
(ee-man-suh-<u>pay</u>-shun)
Setting someone free from the power or control of another person.

IN THE NORTH: CITY LIFE

Most enslaved people in the North worked as butlers, cooks, shipyard workers, and carpenters, although New York, Rhode Island, and New Jersey had large slave populations at work as farmers. In a small-business-based economy, slavery did not make good financial sense, and so it began to die out north of Maryland. There also was a growing feeling in the North that slavery was very wrong.

In 1777 Vermont became the first place to ban slavery, and other northern states soon followed. By 1790 the fast-growing cities of the North were home to many African Americans. In New York and New Jersey some were still enslaved, but many were free. Some grew quite wealthy, such as James Forten—a well-to-do sail maker who used his wealth to work for **emancipation**. People of color felt hopeful that they, too, would finally be able to share in the promise of "life, liberty, and justice for all."

PHYLLIS WHEATLEY (about 1753-1784) was born in Africa and at age seven was sold to a Boston family who taught her alongside their own children. She became one of the most famous poets of her day and wrote plays and poems supporting independence. This modern day painting captures her spirit.

Boston in the late 1700s

OR SOUTH

WHO WERE THEY?

The Maroons

The Spanish word **cimarrón** *means "wild one," and "Maroon" was the nickname for a slave who escaped into the forests and swamps of wild America and started small communities. Many Maroons joined the Seminole Indians in Florida, who welcomed them. Others fled to hidden valleys where they quietly lived out their remaining years.*

Abraham, a Black Seminole

Words to know

▶ **Manumission–**
(man-u-<u>mish</u>-un)
The act of a master freeing a slave.

THE SOUTH: LAND OF COTTON

When George Washington died in 1799, he had a special request in his will. He asked for the **manumission** of all his slaves, and they were given their freedom once his wife Martha died. Washington's act was a shock to many slave owners in the South. With its vast plantations, the South depended on the labor of its slave workforce. How would all the planting, weeding, and harvesting get done?

By the late 1700s there was a new crop thriving in the South—cotton. In 1793 Eli Whitney invented a cotton gin, a machine that would quickly separate cotton fibers from the seeds. Growing cotton quickly became a big business. Cloth factories and mills sprang up in the North and in England.

Cotton would change America in both the North and the South. It would lead to riches for some and misery for many others. Those fluffy little tufts of cotton would help drag the United States into a terrible war.

This painting shows the hard life of a field worker. The cotton gin led to many slaves being moved into the deep South, sold far away from their families.

A cotton plantation in the early 1800s

JUST SAY "NO"

"We will wade to our knees in blood sooner than fail in the attempt"

GABRIEL PROSSER
LEADER OF GABRIEL'S REVOLT IN 1800

By the end of the 1700s, free African Americans were making decent lives for themselves in some places. There were black land owners and even a few black slave-owners, who sometimes bought enslaved families simply to keep them together.

In the North as slavery began to end, it seemed like the Revolution's promise of equality for all *might* be coming true. But in the South the number of slaves and the hardships of their lives were growing.

THE LOUSIANA PURCHASE 1803—FROM FRANCE

SPANISH TERRITORY

THE U.S. IN 1803

SPANISH TERRITORY

Some slave owners made their enslaved workers wear iron collars with bells on the end so sneaking off was impossible.

NO SLAVES	**NORTHERN STATES:** *Vermont, New Hampshire, Rhode Island, Massachusetts (which included Maine), Connecticut*
SLAVERY IS COMING TO AN END	**MID-ATLANTIC STATES:** *New York, New Jersey, Pennsylvania, Delaware, Maryland*
SLAVERY IS PERMITTED	**SOUTHERN STATES:** *Virginia, North Carolina, South Carolina, Georgia, Tennessee, Kentucky*
NO SLAVES	**NORTHERN TERRITORIES:** *The Northwest Ordinance of 1787 made this a free region.*
SLAVERY IS PERMITTED	**SOUTHERN TERRITORIES:** *New areas where slavery was allowed.*

Words to know

▶ **Racism–** (<u>ray</u>-siz-um)
Judging people because of the color of their skin or their place of birth, and putting limits on their ability to succeed.

A GROWING PROBLEM

The United States was expanding its territory. People were pushing into the heartland of the continent, making their way west. There were lots of questions about how to divide up the new land. Would these new territories allow slavery? How would these new places become states? It was getting so complicated!

As the 1700s ended and the new century began, things were unsettled for people of color. For enslaved field hands toiling in the hot sun, gathering their quotas of up to 250 pounds of cotton a day, life had few rewards. Their religion brought them some comfort, but they were getting angry. What could they do?

THE SLAVE REVOLTS
Fighting Back!

Inspired by Bible stories, time and again, enslaved men and women fought back. Sometimes things got so bad they felt they had to turn to violence. There had been many revolts since the early 1700s. GABRIEL PROSSER, an enslaved blacksmith in Virginia, led an army of more than 1,000 slaves in 1800, but a bad storm washed out bridges and flooded roads. Gabriel was captured and killed. In 1831 a dream led NAT TURNER to lead another revolt in Virginia, which set off a sad wave of killings. In the end he, too, failed, but each revolt left slave owners more fearful, and they in turn tried even harder to break black spirits.

Shock waves hit America in 1791, with news of a successful slave revolt led by TOUSSAINT L'OVERTURE in Saint Domingue (now Haiti). In 1804 the birth of a new black nation in the Americas gave hope to enslaved African Americans. L'Overture became a hero to many.

FROM HOPE TO FEAR

By 1804 the northern states had ended slavery. The mid-Atlantic states were phasing it out. In Maryland and Virginia, slaves that had saved money for years by selling crafts or doing odd jobs could buy their freedom, but they had to carry "freedom papers" at all times. These papers proved a person was free, but he or she could still be snatched away for no reason. Free blacks could not vote or speak against whites in a court of law. In some places they could not get married or learn to read. They could be enslaved simply for breaking a law.

In the new southern territories big plantations soon dotted the landscape. Because so many slaves lived there, blacks sometimes outnumbered whites. Plantation owners worked hard to prove they were in charge. Slave uprisings, both large and small, had made many white people fearful of blacks, and years of bad treatment had made blacks distrust and dislike whites. The terrible conditions of the enslaved and the **racism** that kept them that way were problems that began to divide the nation.

1777	1780	1783	1787	1789	1791	1803
VERMONT BECOMES THE FIRST STATE TO BAN SLAVERY.	PENNSYLVANIA STARTS TO FREE ITS SLAVES.	MASSACHUSETTS BANS SLAVERY. BLACK MEN CAN NOW VOTE THERE.	NORTHWEST ORDINANCE BLOCKS SLAVERY IN NORTHERN TERRITORY.	THE U.S. CONSTITUTION BECOMES LAW. BLACKS LOSE SOME RIGHTS.	REBELLION IN HAITI SHOCKS AMERICA.	THE LOUISIANA PURCHASE DOUBLES THE SIZE OF THE U.S.

Nothing was sadder than a slave auction. Skilled men and women fetched the highest prices followed by teenaged boys. This mom was about to be sold and sent away from her daughter.

AM I NOT A PERSON?

"...truth is of no color. God is the father of us all."

FREDERICK DOUGLASS, AN ABOLITIONIST • 1852

Words to know

▶ **Abolition—**
(ab-o-<u>lish</u>-un)
The act of ending slavery.

▶ **Abolitionists—**
(ab-o-<u>lish</u>-un-ists)
People who work to end slavery.

Traveling on foot and wading across rivers so tracking dogs would lose their scent, people risked death on the Underground Railroad.

The Quakers, a religious group, believed that *all* people were created by God. They became one of the first groups to speak out for an end to slavery and help start the **abolition** movement. Other religious groups joined in, but when it came to crying out for freedom, no voices were more moving than those of former slaves. Free black and white abolitionists worked together to help people understand that slavery had to end. They began to speak out in public. They worked to free their people.

ESCAPE TO FREEDOM

As early as the 1820s, enslaved people began to "travel" on the Underground Railroad. It wasn't a train or a tunnel. Instead, it was a series of safe houses and hiding places leading north to help protect runaways. By 1850 brave people like William Still, a black Philadelphian, and other African Americans had helped the "railroad" reach all the way to Canada, where escaped slaves were safe from recapture. Using secret codes and disguises, thousands made their way to freedom, helped by **abolitionists** and free black families along the way.

Fines Summary for HIDALGO, MARIA
Tue Mar 10 10:53:36 PDT 2020

STATUS: OverdueX
TITLE: Fly high! : the story of Bessie C
LOCATION: wsj
AMOUNT: $10.00

Total outstanding fines: $10.00

The Great Abolitionists

Soujourner Truth

SOJOURNER TRUTH (1797-1883) *was a freed slave from New York who claimed she heard heavenly voices urging her to fight slavery. She was a brilliant speaker who opened people's eyes to slavery's sadness and also fought for women's rights.*

Frederick Douglass

FREDERICK DOUGLASS (1817-1895) *escaped from a cruel slavemaster and fled north, where he changed his name, learned to read and write, and began speaking about the horrors of slave life. He started a newspaper,* **The North Star,** *devoted to ending slavery.*

HARRIET TUBMAN (1820-1913) *was a wisp of a woman, but that didn't stop her from escaping from slavery when she was 29. She became known as "Moses" because of her many dangerous trips to the South to help lead more than 300 people to freedom on the Underground Railroad.*

Harriet Tubman

UNCLE TOM'S CABIN

In a time long before television and the Internet, most people knew only what was going on in their own homes and villages. Unless they were living the life of an enslaved person, how could they know what it really was like? Books by former slaves and abolitionist newspapers were widely read. In 1852 Harriet Beecher Stowe, a white abolitionist, decided to write a novel based on true stories about the sadness of slavery. She called it *Uncle Tom's Cabin,* and it quickly became one of America's best-selling books ever. Millions read it, and the book drew an even deeper line between southern slave owners who burned copies of the book and Northerners who wept as they read it.

Words to know

▶ **Discrimination**–
(dis-crim-uh-<u>nay</u>-shun)
Treating people differently because of race, religion, gender, or place of birth.

▶ **Segregation**–
(seg-ruh-<u>gay</u>-shun)
Keeping people of different races or social groups apart.

▶ **Antebellum**–
(ant-ee-<u>bell</u>-um)
The time period just before the Civil War. **Ante** *means* **before** *in Latin, and* **bellum** *means* **war**.

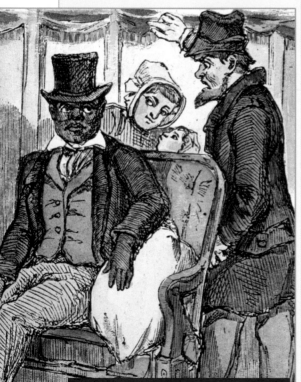

CAUTION!!
COLORED PEOPLE
OF BOSTON, ONE & ALL,
You are hereby respectfully CAUTIONED and advised, to avoid conversing with the
Watchmen and Police Officers
of Boston,
For since the recent ORDER OF THE MAYOR & ALDERMEN, they are empowered to act as
KIDNAPPERS
AND
Slave Catchers,
And they have already been actually employed in KIDNAPPING, CATCHING, AND KEEPING SLAVES. Therefore, if you value your LIBERTY, and the Welfare of the Fugitives among you, Shun them in every possible manner, as so many HOUNDS on the track of the most unfortunate of your race.
Keep a Sharp Look Out for
KIDNAPPERS, and have a
TOP EYE open.
APRIL 24, 1851.

"...I found every door was closed against the colored man in a free state except the jails..."

A FREE BLACK MAN, OHIO • 1827

In 1820 waves of newcomers from Europe started to migrate to America, drawn by the hope of a better life. As a result, free blacks had to compete for jobs and housing with white people who were desperate for work. Skin color began to be used as a way to decide *who* should get jobs and *what* those jobs would be. African Americans began to face growing **discrimination.**

KEEP OUT!

During America's **antebellum** years, people of color began to be turned away from restaurants and told they could not get on certain trains. Black children started getting shut out of white schools. Black city-dwellers ended up moving to parts of town for people of color only. The late 1800s saw the seed of an idea called "separate but equal" begin to take root, but the truth was that black schools and housing were not nearly as good. They were, in truth, NOT equal.

In the North, in places where free blacks and whites had once lived as neighbors, **segregation** began to pull them apart. Black leaders began building their own churches, publishing black newspapers, and forming their own schools. They held their heads high and kept on working for equality. They refused to give up hope.

"Get off at the next stop!" A mom and her daughter look on as a Philadelphia train conductor tells this well-dressed man he must leave—simply because he is black.

After too many beatings and hardships, some enslaved men and women felt they had no choice but to run. Some went north while others headed into the wilds of the unsettled American west. The ones who died trying were said to have "flown back to Africa."

WANTED: RUNAWAYS!

Every year thousands of slaves fled toward freedom. By the mid-1800s free blacks in the South had to carry papers at all times, proving they were free. Without these papers, every black person was assumed to be a runaway. Still people kept running away, so wealthy slave owners set out to stop the escapes. At their urging in 1850, the U.S. Congress passed another and harsher ***Fugitive Slave Law.***

The new laws listed punishments and fines for anyone caught helping escaped slaves. It also stripped free African Americans of their rights because it made it impossible to prove they were free in the first place! Worse, it encouraged some police officers to kidnap free blacks and sell them to slave owners for a reward.

Return to Africa

When Sengbe Pieh was kidnapped in 1839 in Sierra Leone, he vowed to return. He was taken to Cuba and given the name JOSEPH CINQUE. While being moved on a boat called the **Amistad**, he seized the ship in a revolt and tried to sail back to Africa. Cinque and his crew were caught and jailed in Connecticut, but after former U.S. President John Quincy Adams fought for the Africans' freedom, Cinque was freed. He returned to Africa only to find that his entire family was dead.

Other black Americans sailed back to their ancestral homelands with hope of a new start. Some felt that Africa was the only place they would ever be at home. In 1815 a wealthy black businessman, PAUL CUFFEE, led a group to Sierra Leone on Africa's west coast to start a colony. In the 1820s another group formed a second African colony called Liberia, which means "freedom." However, many blacks felt they had become African American. America was now their home too.

A portrait of Cinque

Even in the North, people of color were not safe. The Slave Law drew yet another line between people who supported slavery and those who hated it. And in the new western territories, things were truly a mess.

THE PUSH WEST

"California is the best place for black folks on the globe. All a man has to do is work and he will make money."

PETER BROWN, A BLACK MINER • 1851

When the explorers Lewis and Clark went west in 1807, an African American named YORK went with them. York, Clark's slave, was especially good at dealing with the American Indians. They were often amazed by York's black skin. Some Indians even tried to rub his color off!

Words to know

▶ **Compromise–**
(<u>com</u>-pro-mize)
An agreement to settle an argument in which each party gives up some ground.

An African American gold miner in California shows off his claim.

Cherokee moms proudly hold their babies. Blacks were welcomed into many American Indian nations.

As the United States pushed west, so too did African Americans. Some escaped from slavery to live in hidden valleys and secret hollows. Others joined with American Indians and became valued tribal leaders. People of color went west for the same reason everyone in America did—to make a better life for themselves or their families.

A LINE IS DRAWN

By 1820 America had twelve free states and twelve slave states—an uneasy balance. To keep that balance, the government decided to draw a "line" through the new Louisiana territory. Their decision was called the **Missouri Compromise.** Every new territory added to the North would be free. Everyone to the south would live in slave states. Unfortunately an imaginary line was no match for the growing problem of American slavery.

GOLD RUSH

When a huge amount of gold was found in California in 1848, Americans went wild. Within a year folks were heading west hoping to strike it rich. African Americans were no exception. Moving west, many became fur trappers and shopkeepers on their way to the gold fields. Some settled along the way and became **homesteaders,** and the first all black towns sprang up. The rush of people to California meant a new state was about to be born—along with a new problem.

A YEAR OF CHANGE

In 1850 California came into the Union as a free state. That was the same year that the *Fugitive Slave Law* (see page 27) was written to quiet southern slave owners. The outcry was swift. Northerners, both black and white, were angered by the law. Black leaders tried to get African Americans to rise up, unite as a people and fight for their rights. But in a country that had stripped them of virtually *all* their rights, how could they be heard?

"BLEEDING KANSAS"

The fight over slavery's borders was growing more violent every day, and by 1854 the Kansas Territory had become the scene of a small civil war. Pro-slavery and anti-slavery families began shooting at each other after a new U.S. law passed that said that the people who actually *lived* in a territory would decide whether to allow slavery or not. Soon many of the 8,500 settlers were waving guns and dying in the crossfire. People began to call the territory "Bleeding Kansas," and as gunfire rang out, America headed into some of its darkest days.

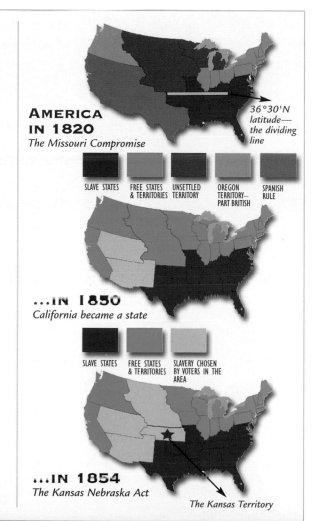

AMERICA IN 1820
The Missouri Compromise

36°30'N latitude— the dividing line

SLAVE STATES | FREE STATES & TERRITORIES | UNSETTLED TERRITORY | OREGON TERRITORY— PART BRITISH | SPANISH RULE

...IN 1850
California became a state

SLAVE STATES | FREE STATES & TERRITORIES | SLAVERY CHOSEN BY VOTERS IN THE AREA

...IN 1854
The Kansas Nebraska Act

The Kansas Territory

Words to know

▶ **Homesteader–**

(<u>home</u>-sted-ur)
A person who settles lawfully on government land, improves it, and in exchange then owns it.

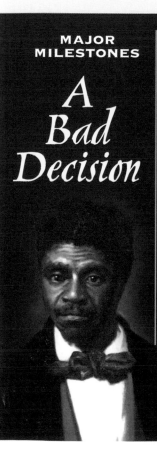

MAJOR MILESTONES

A Bad Decision

Our government is here to protect us, but there have been some unfair, cruel laws that hurt honest, hard-working people. DRED SCOTT (1800-1858), was a Virginia slave who was taken by his owner to Illinois, a state where slavery was against the law. He sued for his freedom based on that fact. In 1856 his case ended up in the Supreme Court, America's highest court.

The Court ruled that Scott was a piece of property, just like a table or chair. The Court said that a slave owner could take his property (slaves) wherever he wanted and they would remain slaves—even if they moved to free states. Folks in the free states were outraged!

THE CIVIL WAR

![decorative pattern]

"...I had rather die than be a slave!"

JOHN COPELAND, JR,
A BLACK ABOLITIONIST, AFTER HIS TRIAL
FOR THE HARPER'S FERRY REVOLT • 1859

Abraham Lincoln was President during our nation's worst crisis—Civil War—a time when people from the same country went to war with one another. Some men even fought against their own kinfolk!

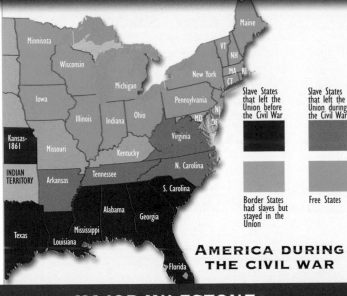

AMERICA DURING THE CIVIL WAR

Slave States that left the Union before the Civil War

Slave States that left the Union during the Civil War

Border States had slaves but stayed in the Union

Free States

MAJOR MILESTONEs
Harper's Ferry

On a Sunday night in October 1859, a white abolitionist, JOHN BROWN, led a group of men to a building in Harper's Ferry, in what is now West Virginia. The government's guns and ammunition were inside. He and his supporters—both black and white—planned to grab the guns, invade the South, and start a war. His plan failed, but his capture and death by hanging caused an uproar in the months leading to the election of a new President.

The days that led up to the start of the **War Between the States** were full of angry speeches, a presidential election, and last-minute attempts to keep America from splitting in two.

In the North people hated the idea of slavery, but in a strange twist, many had become terrible racists. They had been told over and *over* again that black people were not as good as white people. They had heard it so often that many foolishly believed it. In the South many white people believed that black people were like small children—they needed protecting in order to survive. Many untrue beliefs ran deep in these terrible times!

The presidential election of 1860 was a nasty one as the country split over the issue of slavery. Four men ran for office. Abraham Lincoln's name wasn't even on the ballots in the South. What was the point? He was anti-slavery. Some people in the North didn't like him either, but many thought he was the best of the men running. He won with just 40% of the popular vote. His election continued a series of events that changed America forever.

At the start of the war, black men rushed to join the Union army but were turned away. They were finally allowed to enlist in 1863 after the North had suffered some big losses, but were kept in all-black units. This hand-colored photo shows the men of the 4th Colored Infantry in Maryland.

THE UNION BREAKS

With the news of Lincoln's victory, South Carolina made a bold move and became the first state to **secede** from the Union. Soon seven more states joined in and formed the **Confederate States of America**. When a U.S. military base—South Carolina's Fort Sumter—was attacked in April, 1861 by Confederate soldiers, there was no turning back. This was war! In all, twelve states joined the **Confederacy**, determined to keep their slaves no matter what.

Robert E. Lee led the Confederate Army and the Confederate flag became a symbol of struggle for many years to come.

A NEW FREEDOM

At first Lincoln was afraid to end slavery. He had an idea to buy all the slaves from their owners and ship them away to the Caribbean and Latin America, but on New Year's Day in 1863, he did something more meaningful. On that day he issued the **Emancipation Proclamation**, a document that freed every enslaved person in the Confederate States (but not those still enslaved in the North). He hoped to encourage southern slaves to revolt. As news spread, church bells rang in the North, and people wept with joy.

Four million enslaved African Americans would not be officially free until 1865, when America's laws finally changed, but for now the nation battled and bled—fighting to save the Union and put an end to slavery.

Words to know

▶ **Secede–**
(suh-<u>seed</u>)
To withdraw from or pull out.

▶ **Proclamation–**
(prok-luh-<u>may</u>-shun)
A formal public statement or announcement.

▶ **Confederacy–**
(kun-<u>fed</u>-er-uh-see)
The southern states that seceded from the United States in 1861.

DEC. 1860	FEB. 1861	APR. 1861	JULY, 1861	APR. 1862	SEPT.1862	JAN. 1863
S. CAROLINA LEAVES THE UNION AFTER LINCOLN'S ELECTION.	THE CONFEDERATE STATES OF AMERICA IS FORMED.	FORT SUMTER IS ATTACKED BY CONFEDERATE TROOPS.	FIRST BATTLE OF BULL RUN GIVES THE SOUTH A VICTORY.	23,000 ARE DEAD OR WOUNDED IN THE BATTLE OF SHILOH.	26,000 ARE KILLED OR HURT IN THE BATTLE OF ANTIETAM.	EMANCIPATION PROCLAMATION FREES SLAVES IN THE CONFEDERACY.

IN THE COTTON FIELD

THE CHRISTMAS DANCE

THE SALE

THE PARTING
"BUY US TOO"

THE LASH

BLOW FOR BLOW

THE FIGHT DRAGS ON

"We have done a soldier's duty.
Why can't we have a soldier's pay?"

CPL. JAMES HENRY GOODING • 1863

SUSIE KING TAYLOR risked her life traveling with the troops as a nurse.

Many Civil War soldiers had portraits made with a brand new invention—the camera—before going off to fight.

Words to know

▶ **Amendment**
(Uh-<u>mend</u>-mint)
A change or addition to an existing law or rule.

▶ **Assassination–**
(Uh-sass-in-<u>a</u>-shun)
The killing of an important person.

For four terrible years, the Civil War raged on in places like Antietam in Virginia, on the bloody fields of Gettysburg, Pennsylvania, and as far west as Missouri. For a while it seemed like the South might win. In battle after battle, victory went to the Confederate Army.

JOINING IN

After three years of losses, it was time for a change. The North's Union Army let black men join. More than 120,000 proudly enlisted and fought with great courage, yet were paid less than the wages paid to white soldiers. Freedom may have come to African Americans, but equality had not.

Many blacks worked as spies and guides. One couple sent military information by hanging laundry to dry in special patterns—the wife did laundry for a Confederate officer, and her husband was a cook for the Union army. But no matter how hard black people worked, even as they fought and died, they were usually treated poorly.

IN THE SWAMP | FREE! | "STAND UP A MAN!" | "MAKE WAY FOR LIBERTY" | VICTORY! | "HE DIED FOR ME!"

FROM LOSS TO VICTORY

Finally, with help from many ex-slaves who joined the Union army and the dynamic leadership of General William Sherman, the city of Atlanta, Georgia, fell in September of 1864. The war's tide began to turn. A few months later on January 31, 1865, a new law was passed. The **13th Amendment** changed America's Constitution and declared the end of slavery *everywhere* in the United States. As the South faced defeat, their generals made a last, desperate move. They too allowed slaves to join their armies with the promise of freedom if they won. It was too late.

This series of cards was created in 1863. They showed one man's journey from slave to runaway to hero.

President Lincoln is shot by John Wilkes Booth as Lincoln's wife and friends look on in horror.

A FALLEN LEADER

On a fine spring day in April of 1865, General Robert E. Lee and his Confederate Army surrendered at Appomattox Courthouse in Virginia. The war was over! Millions had fought, and more than 600,000 lives had been lost in the struggle.

Five days later a weary President Lincoln sat relaxing, watching a play at Ford's Theater in Washington, DC. Suddenly John Wilkes Booth, a southern actor, burst in and fired a gun! By the next day Lincoln was dead—the first President to lose his life in an **assassination**. Lincoln's body made one last 1,700-mile trip back to Springfield, Illinois—his home town. A nine-car funeral train stopped at cities along the way so people could pay their respects to the fallen leader. All along that sad route, African Americans stood by the train tracks with tear-stained faces, wondering what would happen next.

War Department, Washington, April 20, 1865,
$100,000 REWARD!
THE MURDERER
Of our late beloved President, Abraham Lincoln,
IS STILL AT LARGE.
$50,000 REWARD
$25,000 REWARD
$25,000 REWARD

JULY, 1863	MAR. 1864	SEP-NOV. 1864	JAN. 1865	APR. 9, 1865	APR. 14, 1865
GETTYSBURG BECOMES THE BLOODIEST BATTLE IN U.S. HISTORY.	ULYSSES S. GRANT TAKES CONTROL OF THE UNION ARMY.	ATLANTA FALLS TO THE UNION ARMY. LINCOLN IS ELECTED FOR A SECOND TERM.	13TH AMMENDMENT ABOLISHES SLAVERY IN AMERICA.	GENERAL LEE SURRENDERS AT APPOMATTOX. THE WAR IS OVER.	LINCOLN IS SHOT BY JOHN WILKES BOOTH AND DIES THE NEXT DAY.

HEALING A NATION

> "Glory! Glory, Hallelujah! This is my Betty, for sure! I found you at last!"
>
> **BEN DODSON, REUNITED WITH HIS WIFE AFTER 20 YEARS APART • 1865**

The right to vote was one of the greatest joys for the new freedmen.

Words to know

▶ **Reconstruction**

(re-con-<u>struck</u>-shun)
The years between 1865-1877 when the nation re-united and rebuilt after the Civil War ended.

▶ **Sharecropper**

(<u>share</u>-crop-ur)
A farmer who pays for using a piece of land by paying with a portion of a crop grown on that land.

A sharecropper mom stands proudly before her home and her crops.

The end of slavery changed America completely. In the months after the war ended, African Americans who had labored for unkind masters packed up and moved on. For slaves who had been treated kindly by their owners, the decision to leave was very hard. Still, for most folks an owner's kindness could not compete with the sweet joy of freedom.

The first order of business for many freed slaves was a search for family who had been sold away from them. Wives went looking for husbands. Mothers and fathers went in search of their children. There were happy reunions and some sad times, too, as people learned what had happened to lost loved ones.

HOPE GROWS

The twelve year period following the war is called **Reconstruction**. It was a time of great hope for people of color. Newly freed blacks needed jobs and homes. They wanted to get an education, and with it a chance for a better life. To help them get these things, the U.S. government created a special group called *Freedmen's Bureau,* but just as quickly as it was formed, the bureau's ability to help the former slaves crumbled.

MAR. 1865	NOV. 1865	1868	1870	1870	1872	1877-79
CONGRESS CREATES THE FREEDMEN'S BUREAU TO HELP FREED SLAVES.	MISSISSIPPI PASSES "BLACK CODES" TO TAKE AWAY RIGHTS.	14TH AMENDMENT DECLARES ALL PEOPLE BORN IN THE U.S. ARE CITIZENS.	15TH AMENDMENT GIVES BLACK MEN THE RIGHT TO VOTE.	FIRST AFRICAN AMERICAN IS ELECTED U.S. SENATOR.	FREEDMEN'S BUREAU IS CLOSED.	LAST U.S TROOPS LEAVE THE SOUTH.

Forty Acres and a Mule

*After the war the government controlled a lot of land in the South. In January of 1865, an 80-mile wide, 245-mile long tract of land was set aside for newly freed slaves. The head of each family got 40 acres of land and a mule to help with the work. About 40,000 freed people began farming, but within a few months their land was taken away. A new President, Andrew Johnson, decided to forgive the Confederate soldiers and gave them back their land. Many former slaves ended up back at work in fields that were once again owned by whites, this time as **sharecroppers**—a very difficult way to live.*

A sharecropper might be free by law, but not by way of life. It was so hard to make ends meet that some called it "a second form of slavery."

Read about Hiram Revels the first black U.S. Senator on page 80.

Isaac and Rosa were two freed children who proudly went off to school in Louisiana.

HOPE FADES

The early days of Reconstruction saw the building of churches, banks, schools, and colleges for blacks and whites in the South. The 15th Ammendment to the U.S. Constitution allowed black men to vote and run for political office, and by 1870 Hiram Revels, the first African American senator, went to Washington. But just because the government *said* that black people were now equal to whites did not make it true in the minds of many white people. Hatefully, they vowed to fight in any way they could—even if it meant burning a school or beating a person to death. Truly terrible times were coming again.

Learning to read and write was very important to newly freed blacks of all ages. Classrooms were filled with youngsters sitting next to grandparents, all learning side by side.

WORSE THAN SLAVERY

*"They had dragged and beat us along...
I said, Lord o'mercy, don't kill my child!"*

**HARRIET HERNANDEZ,
DESCRIBING HER SECOND KLAN ATTACK • 1871**

How different our nation's story might have been if Abraham Lincoln had lived! Andrew Johnson and Ulysses S. Grant, the Presidents that followed Lincoln, were not strong leaders. All the good that had come about with the end of slavery soon began to slip away.

A TERRIBLE HATE

In the early days of Reconstruction, black men won elections at the local, state, and national levels, but even those elected to the highest offices were treated poorly. Black U.S. Senators and Congressmen in Washington could not stay in hotels or eat in most restaurants.

Throughout the South, as freed slaves tried to claim their piece of the American dream, they found their way blocked. There were constant outbreaks of violence in the South as white mobs attacked black students or burned down black churches. African Americans tried to get lawmakers to stop the violence, but the sad truth was that America's justice system was unjust when it came to people of color.

THE WHITE "HATE" GROUPS
The Klan

Dressed in robes to hide their bodies and pillowcases to mask their faces, the men of the Ku Klux Klan were a group of hateful bullies. Started by a group of bitter ex-Confederate Army soldiers, the Klan's aim was to destroy any chance for African Americans to gain equality in America. They started riots and killed innocent people for no reason. They burned homes and schools. Much of their violence was aimed at successful blacks or those who were active in politics. More than 4,500 African Americans were killed by Klan mobs in the South simply because they "bothered" a white person.

JIM CROW LAW.
UPHELD BY THE UNITED STATES
SUPREME COURT.

Statute Within the Competency of
the Louisiana Legislature and
Railroads—Must Furnish Separate Cars for Whites and
Blacks.
—The Supreme
—d by Jus-
tion-

Klan attacks could happen at any time and for no reason, as this family was about to discover.

THE BLACK CODES

By the 1870s laws that had given black people equal rights changed in many places with new rules called the **Black Codes**. Voting was almost impossible because of high poll taxes—fees that had to be paid in order to cast a vote. There were also tests "for blacks only." In one town, in order to vote, black citizens had to be able to tell how many soap bubbles there were in a bar of wet soap!

The U.S. Constitution allows each state to decide how things should be run within that state, so southern states wrote harsh laws to keep blacks apart from whites. In 1892 a man named Homer Plessy was tossed in jail for sitting in a "white" train car in Louisiana. Plessy was 7/8 white and 1/8 black, but even a drop of African blood legally made a person black. In 1896 the United States Supreme Court heard his case—**Plessy v. Ferguson**—and decided that states *could* separate blacks from whites. Segregation was now officially legal.

In the South, people of color had to go to separate schools, pray in separate churches, ride in the backs of buses, and use inferior restrooms. Many blacks knew that "separate but equal" was a big lie. Tired of living in fear, some gave up, packed up, and moved away.

MAJOR MILESTONES
Meet Jim Crow

In the days before TV and movies, people went to live shows. Minstrel shows—with singing, dancing, and joke-telling—were a big hit, especially in the North.

In the 1830s a white singer smeared charcoal on his face, pretended he was black, and did a silly dance while singing a ditty called "Jump Jim Crow." White audiences howled with laughter, and the name of that character became an unkind way to refer to African Americans. In the years after Reconstruction, laws to keep blacks apart from whites became known as Jim Crow laws.

For more than 60 years Jim Crow laws were a way of life in the South. There were now two Americas—one for whites, one for blacks. When the two mixed, it often led to bloodshed.

NORTH CAROLINA LAW
White Patrons Please Seat From Front
Colored Patrons Please Seat From Rear
NO SMOKING

Buffalo Soldiers

THE PIONEERS

*"When I landed on the soil, I looked at the ground
and I said this is free ground.
Then I looked at the heavens, and I said
<u>that</u> is a free and beautiful heaven..."*

**JOHN SOLOMON LEWIS, ON HIS ARRIVAL
IN KANSAS IN THE 1870s**

Constant attacks by the Ku Klux Klan and other white **supremacists** made life dangerous in the South. The unsettled lands of the West offered a chance for black men and women to build new lives. The government was offering land to people willing to work, so between 1865 and 1880 more than 40,000 African Americans crammed onto jam-packed ships, sailed up the Mississippi River, and headed west.

THE EXODUSTERS

Many African Americans fled to Kansas, a state that welcomed them. They were nicknamed the *Exodusters* from the Bible story of Exodus, and they played a big role in the settling of America's frontiers. They staked land claims, worked hard, and in time started all-black frontier towns—places like Nicodemus, Kansas, which grew into a lively village of 200 people.

NAT LOVE (1854-1921) was also known as Deadwood Dick. He was one of the West's most famous cowboys. Love said black cowboys were treated the same as whites "as long as our money lasted."

The Buffalo Soldiers

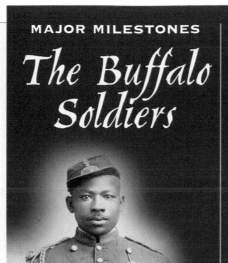

In 1867 when Cheyenne Indians first saw a group of soldiers with dark skin, curly hair, and a fearless fighting style, they were reminded of their sacred buffalo, so they called the men Buffalo Soldiers. The name stuck.

These men (and a few women too) came from different walks of life. Some were former slaves while others had fought in the Civil War. As the U.S. government took more and more native lands, and the Indians tried to protect their property, Buffalo Soldiers saved settlers from attack. The soldiers rode with stagecoaches and hunted down outlaws. They guarded the railroad that was being built to link the nation. Still, in spite of their bravery, they were often treated terribly by white soldiers, given inferior rations and old horses. Discrimination had followed them out West.

Words to know

▶ **Supremacists**

(soo-<u>prem</u>-a-sists) *People who believe they are better than others because of a particular trait, such as skin color, culture, or religion.*

This 1887 family portrait shows the Speese family of Nebraska, once enslaved, now sitting proudly in front of their little sod house on the prairie.

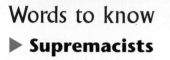

DUNG FIRES AND FREEDOM

Life in the West was hard, and new settlers often found that their land claims were for acres with no trees. They built houses made of sod—bricks made from slabs of grass and soil—and had to cook

Nicodemus, Kansas in 1885

on fires made from buffalo dung, but given a choice between hard work on the prairie or life in the deep South, the West was much better. By the end of the 1800s, there were nearly fifty black towns from Kansas to California.

THE BLACK COWBOYS

There was one line of work in which many African-American men gained great respect and a degree of equality with whites—raising cattle. In the years after the Civil War, skilled horsemen headed west to Texas, Nebraska, and Missouri. In the heyday of the great cattle ranches, about one quarter of all the cowboys were black.

BLACK VOICES

"There are two ways of exerting one's strength: one is pushing down, the other is pulling up."

BOOKER T. WASHINGTON

Words to know

▶ **Agriculture–**
(ag-ri-cul-chur)
The growing of crops and raising of animals.

▶ **Lynching–**
(lin-ching)
An attack on a person that usually ended with the victim's death by hanging. Some people were lynched for things as small as failing to move out of the way of a white person.

As the 1800s came to an end and a new century began, African Americans hoped that things might get better.

SPEAKING UP

By 1900 the African American community was growing stronger. There were schools and universities teaching **agriculture** and trade skills. Black churches were at the heart of every black neighborhood. They were sources of hope for the spirit and helping hands for those in need of food, medical care, or simply friendship. Self-help groups and clubs also gave support and formed a network of caring.

Black people fought for the right to go to law school and medical school. They opened shops, built hospitals, started banks and businesses, and created their own wonderful forms of entertainment. Even though they did most of this apart from white America, they slowly changed the way the entire nation worked, lived, and played. As some gained success, they became role models for other African Americans—proof that even in a segregated country there was hope for a better future. Still, life was often dangerous and sometimes even deadly for people of color.

Students learn about Jamestown in a class at Tuskegee Institute in the 1890s. In addition to learning trades such as cooking or furniture making, students also studied English, history, science, and math.

BOOKER T. WASHINGTON (1856-1915) was born into slavery on a small farm in Virginia. After emancipation and time spent working in coal mines, he was determined to get an education. He studied at Hampton Institute and in 1881 founded Tuskegee Institute in Alabama, which became a center for black education. His book, UP FROM SLAVERY, inspired many.

ENOUGH IS ENOUGH

Booker T. Washington believed that he could make things better for his people by working *with* the system, even if it *was* unfair. Other black leaders did not share his beliefs. New crimes against black people were becoming more common. Horrible **lynchings** and other cruel attacks made many black people realize that they *had* to do something. They *had* to take action.

In September of 1909, the **National Association for the Advancement of Colored People (NAACP)** was born, led by W.E.B. Du Bois and Ida Wells Barnett. The NAACP's goal was to change things—to serve as a loud and powerful voice that would make sure that *every* American learned about black people's suffering at the hands of hateful racists. Through their magazine, **The Crisis,** the NAACP made sure the whole world knew about the violent lynchings of innocent men and women in the South. For the next century the NAACP would play a huge role in the long, difficult, often deadly struggle for equality.

IDA WELLS BARNETT (1862-1931) was a teacher and writer. After three of her friends were lynched, she made it her life's goal to stop the senseless violence. She wrote books on the subject and gave moving speeches all over the United States and in Europe.

Skilled Job or College Degree?

One of the most intense arguments of the early 1900s was about education. On one side sat BOOKER T. WASHINGTON, who believed that the best way for African Americans to get ahead was by learning agricultural and technical skills. At his Tuskegee University, students studied things such as furniture-making and machine repair. He firmly believed that segregation was a fact of life, and it was best to accept it and learn to live with it. On the other side of the debate sat W.E.B. DU BOIS, who argued that black minds had to be challenged in order to produce the next generation of great leaders. Du Bois believed that blacks deserved to stand shoulder to shoulder with whites in ALL walks of life.

W.E.B. DU BOIS (1868-1963) grew up in Massachusetts and became the first black person to get an advanced degree from Harvard University. He became a guiding force in the NAACP—a powerful civil rights group. He spent his life angrily fighting against America's color barriers and eventually moved to Africa.

41

HEADING NORTH

"To die from the bite of frost is far more glorious than at the hands of a mob.... Get out of the South."

**THE CHICAGO DEFENDER,
A BLACK NEWSPAPER • 1917**

Over and over and over again, the same terrible things kept happening. Violence in the South was growing worse. Lynchings led to **riots**. Riots led to many deaths. Black homes were burned, and work was hard to find. In the North there were decent jobs and a chance for a fresh beginning.

ON THE MOVE

The year 1910 marked the start of what came to be called the ***Great Migration***. Over the next thirty years almost two million African Americans packed up and moved away from the South. There were jobs to be had in the big cities up North—in the iron and steel mills, on the railroad, and in the factories. Philadelphia, New York City, Chicago and other big cities saw their black populations quickly grow. Discrimination was still widespread, and African Americans usually ended up living in blacks-only neighborhoods with the worst jobs. In the North a black man could vote, and schools were better, but best of all, life was safer. At least it was at first...

Car loaded, this young boy's family is ready to move North.

1898	1905	1909	1910	1917-18	1919
BLACK TROOPS HEAD TO CUBA TO FIGHT IN THE SPANISH-AMERICAN WAR.	THE NIAGARA MOVEMENT IS FORMED BY LEADING BLACK CITIZENS.	THE NAACP IS STARTED TO FIGHT VIOLENCE AND RACISM.	THE GREAT MIGRATION BEGINS. THE URBAN LEAGUE IS FORMED.	AMERICA ENTERS WORLD WAR I. 365,000 BLACKS SERVE IN THE ARMED FORCES.	MORE THAN 20 VIOLENT RACE RIOTS OCCUR. WORKERS GROW MORE OUTSPOKEN.

The "Great" War

In 1917 America found itself pulled into a huge war in Europe. More than 350,000 African American soldiers and 1,400 officers sailed across the Atlantic Ocean to serve their country. Most soldiers were forced to work as laborers, but in spite of that, one group— the "Harlem Hell Fighters"—had the best record in the U.S. Army. They were warmly welcomed by the people of France, and black soldiers won France's highest military award for bravery and medals for valor. When these soldiers returned to the U.S.A. after the war ended, the sting of racism felt especially bad because the world had changed during the war years. War also changed the way black Americans saw themselves—as heroes who had helped bring peace.

France's highest military honor.

"SUMMERS OF RED"

Sadly, racial violence followed the migrants as they moved north. As big cities grew more crowded, there were housing and job shortages. When African Americans began to speak out for equal rights, some white people reacted badly. Things were tense. Often a riot would start over something small, and within hours white gangs were swarming around the streets, burning homes, and beating any black person who got in their way.

There were so many riots in the summer of 1919 that it became known as the **Summer of Red**. Hundreds died, yet African Americans were willing to fight for what was rightfully theirs. America's cities were going to *have* to change or be destroyed. Through it all they clung to the hope that somehow life would improve.

After a riot in Chicago in 1919, all that is left is the ashes of some homes. This scene was repeated in dozens of cities, from Florida to Washington D.C. to as far west as Nebraska.

43

WE WANT OUR RIGHTS!

"We have come now to the turning point of the Negro...changed from the cringing weakling, and transformed into full grown men."

MARCUS GARVEY

The 1920s were a fast-paced time. Railroads criss-crossed the country. Cars came off the assembly lines of factories in Detroit, and ships sailed America's rivers. Radios had been invented, and with the flick of a dial, you could hear the world's news or the sounds of music. Movie theaters offered an escape from day to day chores. But trouble lay ahead for many of America's workers.

WORKERS WANTED

Black people could find jobs, but those jobs were often the hardest, hottest, or most dangerous. By the 1920s all across America, workers were forming labor **unions** to get their bosses to treat them fairly. One way they did this was by going out on **strike**. As Americans gathered around their radios, they often heard news about union work stoppages that had led to violence. Unfortunately most unions kept black workers out.

COLORED WOMEN FORM LABOR UNION

WOODBURY, N. J., June 11. — A "Domestics' Union" has been formed in this city by the Colored help, the headquarters being in the southern end of the city. Prices have been fixed which are to be strictly adhered to, as many housewives can attest.

The new schedule went into effect yesterday morning by the wash women, who demand $2 per day, or from 8 in the morning to 4 in the afternoon, including breakfast and lunch. The former price was $1.50. Regular servants will give a week's "notice," and those who have been receiving $5 per week, are to insist on $8, with one afternoon a week off, and every other Sunday and "company" two nights each week. Girls acting in the capacity of child's nurse are not connected with the organization, but have been urged to ask for more than they are getting.

Words to know

▶ **Union**–
(<u>yoon</u>-yun)
A group of workers who organize to fight unfair labor practices.

▶ **Strike**–
Stopping work for a period of time to protest unfair practices.

MARY CHURCH TERRELL (1863-1954) devoted her life to fighting for the rights of women. In 1896 she became the first president of the National Association of Colored Women. She kept working into her 80s to end segregation .

Black is Beautiful

"Black men, you were once great. You shall be great again!" With a voice "like thunder from heaven," Jamaican-born MARCUS GARVEY urged people of color to be proud of their African roots. Garvey started the THE UNIVERSAL NEGRO IMPROVEMENT ASSOCIATION, which worked for economic freedom for blacks. He started a shipping company—the Black Star Line, published a newspaper and opened restaurants and shops. In 1927 the U.S. government accused Garvey of using the mail to cheat people. Some historians believe this was done because Garvey was gaining too much power. He was sent to prison on shaky evidence and was ordered to leave America when he got out of jail, but his message of black pride had taken root.

MARCUS GARVEY (1887-1940) was one of the many thousands who moved to America from the West Indies. These newcomers had a big effect on black culture. Garvey's organization had the largest membership of any African American group at the time.

A BLACK BROTHERHOOD

In the 1920s railroads were how most people traveled long distances. Since railroad jobs were one of the few jobs they could get, some African Americans worked as train porters—the people who served food and took care of passengers' needs. Porters worked more than 400 hours a month, much of it unpaid. To protest, the porters started the first black labor union, the **Brotherhood of Sleeping Car Porters,** and by the mid-1930s managed to make some gains to earn fairer wages.

BLACK CITY LIFE

African Americans were getting by, thanks to the hard work of the **NAACP** and the **Urban League**—a group that helped city-dwellers deal with the problems they faced. Still it was hard to find housing since segregation laws limited where blacks could live. In Cleveland, Ohio, 90 percent of the city's black people lived in one small area. Two-thirds of New York City's black population lived in Harlem, but things were happening in Harlem…things that would soon be heard around the world.

ASA PHILIP RANDOLPH (1889-1954) was the man who led the railroad workers in their quest for better wages.

PULLMAN Compartment Cars
CINCINNATI, INDIANAPOLIS, CHICAGO.

INTERIOR OF DINING CARS ON THE CINCINNATI, HAMILTON & DAYTON R.R.

Porters, some of whom had college degrees, carried luggage, shined shoes, served food, and cleaned the train cars for people with less education!

45

Ethel Waters was a glorious singer and fabulous actress.

JOSEPHINE BAKER (1906-1975) *danced, sang, and joked her way to fame. She was the first black female entertainer to break down the walls of race and became a huge star. Baker moved to Paris to escape racism. She wrote, "The Eiffel Tower looked very different from the Statue of Liberty, but what did that matter? What was the good of having the statue without the liberty?"*

Walking down the streets of Harlem in the 1920s, you could almost feel the energy and excitement in the air. Music spilled out from both big night clubs and tiny apartment windows. Artists sculpted and painted, and bookstores displayed works by gifted black writers. Many felt that New York City's Harlem was the center of the cultural universe, and it was here that the years from 1920-1930 became known as the *Jazz Age*.

HARLEM'S RENAISSANCE

"I am not tragically colored. There is no great sorrow dammed up in my soul, nor lurking behind my eyes. I do not mind at all."

ZORA NEALE HURSTON

PAUL ROBESON (1898-1954) *was a brilliant scholar/athlete, who gave up a career as a lawyer to become a singer and actor. He went on to use his fame to work for civil rights.*

Bill Robinson

EDWARD "DUKE" ELLINGTON (1899-1974) was one of the greatest jazz musicians ever— a keyboard genius, composer, and conductor who won many awards and honors.

Lena Horne

Cab Calloway

Dancer Bill "Bojangles" Robinson, singer Lena Horne, and band-leader Cab Calloway were favorites of both black and white audiences.

"THE NEW NEGRO"

Music and storytelling had always been a big part of African life. In the days of slavery, singing helped to pass the time, and stories of life in Mother Africa helped people cling to their roots. As black families flocked to the cities in the 1920s, something special happened. Marcus Garvey's message of black pride—"the new Negro"—had touched many African Americans. W.E.B. DuBois and others at the NAACP were earning respect in the fight for civil rights. The result was the ***Harlem Renaissance***, an outpouring of great talent in the arts, theater, music, and writing.

Read all about ZORA NEALE HURSTON and LANGSTON HUGHES, two brilliant writers, on page 74.

Vibrant paintings such as JACOB LAWRENCE'S "The Library," captured the energy of the Jazz Age.

Words to know

▶ **Renaissance**—
(<u>ren</u>-uh-santz)
A time of new interest in culture—art, music, theater, and writing.

DREAM DEFERRED
BY LANGSTON HUGHES

What happens to a dream deferred?
Does it dry up
like a raisin in the sun?
Or fester like a sore—
and then run?
Does it stink like
rotten meat?
Or crust and sugar
over—like a syrupy
sweet?
Maybe it just sags
like a heavy load.
Or does it explode?

COTTON CLUB NIGHTS

Harlem became the "in" place to go. Wealthy white people drove uptown to swanky nightclubs where black musicians made music, the likes of which they had never heard. They flocked to the *Cotton Club* to see the beautiful brown-skinned showgirls or *Connie's Inn* with its marvelous musicians, but these were clubs for whites only. Black guests were not allowed in, so they started their own clubs where the music was often even better!

47

From the very beginning, enslaved Africans had a secret weapon to help them face hard times—music! It was also a way to "talk" to other slaves without a master knowing. In song, they planned secret meetings and even escapes. Music helped them survive.

ALL THAT JAZZ

*"One of these mornings bright and fair,
I'm gonna lay down my heavy load.
Gonna kick my wings and cleave the air,
I'm gonna lay down my heavy load"*

"THERE IS A BALM IN GILEAD" • A NEGRO SPIRITUAL

MAKING MUSIC

Songs of Faith

As they worked in the fields, African Americans sang songs based on African rhythms to help pass the time. They sang with a "call" and "response" pattern. Someone would sing a line, and the rest of the group would reply. Words came from old folk tales or Bible stories, set to tapped or clapped beats. Some uplifting songs grew into a type of music called SPIRITUALS—*songs about faith in God. In time, more of the music of the fields made its way into church. The word* GOSPEL *means "good news," and spirituals became a big part of prayer meetings.*

Singing for a few short hours helped a person forget about how hard life was.

Go down, Moses
(Let my people go!)

Ladies sang the Blues. These were some of the greatest (from left to right): BILLIE HOLIDAY, GERTRUDE "MA" RAINEY, and BESSIE SMITH.

FEELING "BLUE"

Music and work always seemed to go hand in hand. As enslaved crews built roads and worked along the Mississippi River, they sang slow, sad songs. After the Civil War ended, the songs of the fields mixed with the songs of the road crews and became known as the **blues**. These were songs of sadness—of hard luck and lost love. By the 1890s the blues had spread all across the country.

Some of the best blues singers were women—proof that when it came to music, we *were* all created equal. To this day the blues are still a big part of music. Whenever you hear a really sad love song, you are most likely hearing the blues.

TIME FOR RAGTIME

Not all black music was sad. Around 1900 a new sound hit America. It was piano-based, and it had a bouncy beat. People described the melody as being a little "ragged," so the music became known as **ragtime**. It was lively and modern-sounding, and for 20 years it was America's favorite music. (You can read more about it on page 72.)

JAZZING THINGS UP

Music from Europe was all about the melody. African music was all about rhythm and multiple beats. When African Americans played their "call-and-response" music, they liked to make up their melodies—to improvise—rather than following note-for-note compositions like Europe's musicians did. This new music—a combination of African and European sounds— grew into **jazz**.

Jazz became a huge hit when African Americans brought their music to Europe during World War I. People there loved this exciting new sound. By the 1920s jazz was everywhere! African Americans had given the world a brand-new beat.

As white audiences came to see and hear great black musicians, they left in awe. More than anything else, music began to break down the huge walls that racism had built.

The Jitterbug was one of America's favorite dance crazes.

Here are some of the 1930s coolest, hippest orchestras.

"HIS HI-DE-HIGHNESS OF HO-DE-HO
CAB CALLOWAY *and his* **COTTON CLUB ORCHESTRA**

IN PERSON
"The Sepia Swing Sensation"
COUNT BASIE *and his* **ORCHESTRA**

trumpet
LOUIS *"Satchmo"* **ARMSTRONG**
and his Great Orchestra
Star of STAGE-SCREEN RADIO
Decca Recording Artists

LOUIS ARMSTRONG (1901-1971) had a big grin and an even bigger talent. He was one of jazz's founding fathers. His nickname was "Satchmo." As a boy, he had lots of nicknames which referred to the size of his very large mouth. "Gatemouth," and "Satchelmouth" were two favorites.

MAKING MUSIC

It's Swingtime!

Because the music made you want to swing and sway, by the 1930s SWING had become the hottest sound in town. Swing was music that made you dance—a mix of African rhythm and European-style orchestras. As big band horns blew, folks of all colors all across the nation grabbed a dance partner and let loose.

ELLA FITZGERALD (1917-1996) was a jazz superstar and singing sensation.

49

A SPORTING CHANCE

"A life is not important except in the impact it has on other lives."

— JACKIE ROBINSON

JOSH GIBSON (1911-1947) was one of baseball's greatest sluggers. He hit more than 800 home runs, but his feat was not rewarded because he played in the Negro leagues.

The HOMESTEAD GRAYS were one of the greatest teams ever, anywhere, in any league, with several future hall-of-famers—Josh Gibson, Buck Leonard, and Jamie "Cool Papa" Bell. Between 1938 and 1948 they won nine league championships.

By the 1920s sports were a huge part of American life. Folks adored their favorite teams and players, and no game captured America's heart quite like baseball. In baseball's earliest days black and white men had played together, but in 1887 black players were banned, so they formed a league of their own. Still, plenty of people (even some white baseball team owners) knew that black ball players were some of the most talented athletes around.

LEROY "SATCHEL" PAIGE (1906-1982) was a legend—a beanpole-thin man with a great sense of humor. Many say he was the greatest pitcher ever. He got his nickname because as a kid he carried luggage at the local train station. In 1948 at the age of 42, he finally got to play in the major leagues. One night 78,382 fans came to watch him pitch—a night-game attendance record that has never been broken.

THE NEGRO LEAGUES

Andrew "Rube" Foster—a great ball player and an even better organizer—was the father of black baseball. In the 1920s he gathered the top black ball players into an eight team league that played in cities with large African American populations.

Hard economic times in the early 1930s saw the league break up. In 1934 the league was reborn and went on to produce some of the most dazzling players ever to swing a bat or throw a strike. In 1947, when a white manager named Branch Rickey needed a ballplayer to help his team, he looked to the Negro Leagues to find a star. That ballplayer—Jackie Robinson—would make history.

CROSSING THE COLOR LINE

Jackie Robinson had it all. He was a great athlete, but he was also a man of quiet dignity and determination. In April of 1947, as Robinson stepped up to first base with the all-white Brooklyn Dodgers, boos and curses filled the air. Jackie showed the world what dignity meant. He let his bat talk for him and went on to become the Rookie of the Year and to lead his team to five World Series. Baseball had become **integrated.** Soon, other great black athletes would get to show white sports fans just how good they were.

JACKIE ROBINSON (1919-1972) received death threats. Umpires called him out even when he was safe. Often he could not stay in the same hotels as the rest of his team, but for ten years he led by example and paved the way for other black athletes.

Jackie ROBINSON
second base BROOKLYN DODGERS

VICTORY!

Black athletes quickly became symbols of hope to African Americans. If baseball or track or boxing could become integrated— if black athletes could share their huge talents with the world—maybe one day checking into *any* hotel or sitting *anywhere* on a bus would be a reality for *every* person of color in America. It may have only been a game, but sports were leading the way to integration in other walks of life.

J.C. "JESSE" OWENS (1913-1980) was a star athlete in college.

ALTHEA GIBSON (1927-2003) was the first black woman to play on the world tennis tour and won many events. Because she broke down color barriers, she is often called the female Jackie Robinson.

GREAT FEATS
Pride of the Nation

One of the most evil people of all time was a German leader named Adolf Hitler. He believed that white people were a master race and set out to destroy everyone else. In 1936 the Olympic Games were held in Berlin, Germany, with Hitler as the host. JESSE OWENS, an African-American track star, set off to prove Hitler wrong. He went on to beat Hitler's "master race" and won four gold medals. Owens returned to America a hero, but after a ticker-tape parade he still had to ride the freight elevator to attend a party in his honor at a New York hotel. Nothing had changed…yet.

Words to know

▶ **Integrated**— (in-tuh-grate-id) Mixing racial or religious groups in a community.

Something terrible happened in the 1930s. Much of the world was hit by hard economic times called the **Great Depression**. Many lost their jobs and could not feed their families. Leaders in Germany, Italy, and Japan who wanted more power took advantage of the world's unrest by attacking neighboring countries. Soon the world was dragged into war.

WORLD WAR II BEGINS

One by one, the world's nations sent their soldiers off to battle, but as African Americans signed up to fight, they found themselves stuck in kitchens, boiler rooms, and laundries—rarely in combat. Black soldiers had proven their bravery time and time again in past wars, so as this new war loomed, they vowed to **desegregate** the armed forces so that they could serve their country in a meaningful way. In June 1941, President Franklin D. Roosevelt issued **Executive Order 8804,** which stated that government agencies could not discriminate based on race. It took many years to make it actually happen, but black soldiers still found ways to be heroes.

NONE BUT THE BRAVE

"...we were the only fighter group in the entire Air Force that did not lose a bomber to enemy action. Oh, we were in demand!"

COLEMAN YOUNG, TUSKEGEE AIRMAN

USN-702

"above and beyond the call of duty"

DORIE MILLER
Received the Navy Cross at Pearl Harbor, May 27, 1942

GREAT FEATS

A Hero's Story

On a quiet Sunday morning on December 7, 1941, Japan attacked the U.S. naval base at Pearl Harbor. As bombs exploded, U.S. Navy cook DORIE MILLER dragged his wounded commander to safety, then grabbed a ship's gun and shot down several enemy aircraft. What was amazing was that combat positions were not open to black sailors. Miller had no formal training! Sadly, Miller died later in the war when his next ship was hit by a torpedo. To honor him in 1973 the Navy launched the USS Miller.

The Tuskegee Airmen

One of the first great steps for black equality came about with a group of men who proved that blacks were the equals of whites when it came to leadership and ability. Trained at Tuskegee Institute, these gifted flyers were part of one of the first squadrons to have black officers. THE TUSKEGEE AIRMEN flew more than 1,500 missions, shot down 409 enemy aircraft, sunk a destroyer, and bombed hundreds of ground targets to smithereens without losing a single plane. News of their bravery as fighter-escorts for the big bombers spread, and soon the airmen became legends.

THE FIGHT OF THEIR LIVES

The bombing of Pearl Harbor pushed America into war against Germany and Japan. Soldiers and sailors boarded ships to Europe or Asia, and nearly one million African Americans were among them. Many served as drivers or laborers. They drove trucks through enemy fire, bringing supplies that kept American troops fed and armed. They built airstrips and bridges, and without them the army would have come to a grinding halt. But as some African-American soldiers saw first-hand, German prisoners of war were often treated better than our own black soldiers.

FROM WAR TO PEACE TO WAR

The war raged on for almost four years, from 1941 until peace came in August of 1945. African Americans had fought bravely and made some gains in their fight for equality. There were now black officers and pilots, but for most, the war's end meant a slide back into the same awful segregation that had existed before World War II.

The joy of victory quickly gave way to bad feelings between America and the Soviet Union—an uneasy time known as the ***Cold War***. The years after World War II would bring big changes to the world...and especially to black America.

BENJAMIN O. DAVIS was the first black General—the highest rank in the Army.

BLACK HERITAGE

Benjamin O. Davis, Sr.

32 USA

Words to know

▶ **Desegregate**—
(dee-seg-ruh-gate)
Allow members of all races and ethnic groups to work, go to school, and live together.

War and women went hand in hand. Overseas, black nurses fought for the right to help wounded soldiers of all colors recover. At home black women welded ships, built airplanes, and helped keep America's factories running.

53

WE SHALL OVERCOME

The fight for equality ended up in the highest court in the land. Two lawyers, THURGOOD MARSHALL (1908-1993) and CONSTANCE BAKER MOTLEY (1921-2005) spent years in court fighting to desegregate the schools. Read more on page 80.

In the late 1940s, a group of parents in South Carolina went to the school board to complain. There were more than 6,500 African-American students in the county and fewer than 2,400 white students, yet there were thirty school buses for white students and not a single bus for black children. Does that seem fair? Some African-American students were walking nine miles just to get to school! When the black parents asked for a few school buses, they were rudely turned down. It was time to fight back. The whole "separate but equal" school system was a lie. It had to change. But how?

Change did not come easily to schools in the South. Even first graders faced angry mobs who screamed and threw eggs at them! To protect black children from harm in some places, soldiers with guns were brought in to patrol school yards. It took many, many years until people everywhere finally accepted integrated schools.

BROWN AND THE BOARD OF EDUCATION

Black parents in other states also took their complaints to the NAACP. A group of talented lawyers got together and went to work using existing laws to push for change.

Laws against discrimination had finally ended segregation in the Armed Forces. Baseball was integrated. Now it was time to change the schools. It took years of long courtroom battles, but finally in 1954 a case called **Brown v. the Board of Education of Topeka** ended up at the Supreme Court, the highest court in America. The court ruled that black and white children should be allowed to go to school together, but the story was far from over.

Black riders had to pay the fare at the front, then leave the bus and walk outside to the back. Bus drivers would sometimes pull away before the passenger could reach the back door.

I Will Not Move

Sometimes big events begin with the smallest things. As ROSA PARKS (1913-2006), *a seamstress at a department store in Montgomery, Alabama, rode home from work on December 1, 1955, she found herself being ordered to give her seat to a white man. Mrs. Parks, an active member of the NAACP, made a bold move she had been planning for some time. She refused to budge. She was pulled from the bus and arrested. The NAACP and other black groups sprang into action against the bus company with a* **boycott**. *Rosa Parks—quiet and soft-spoken, yet determined— helped lead the way to change.*

Mrs. Parks was arrested and fingerprinted by a police officer.

Words to know

▶ **Boycott–**
(boy-cot)
Refusing to buy things from a business in order to force them to change their ways.

A LONG WALK

How *do* you make people listen if they refuse to hear? If it is a business, you can hurt them by doing something so they cannot make money. That was the idea behind the **Montgomery Bus Boycott**. After Rosa Parks' arrest, black leaders held a one-day bus boycott that grew into a year-long protest. Some people had to walk twelve miles a day to get to work, but they didn't care. Others formed car pools.

The bus company lost 65 percent of its riders and had to lay off drivers. White businesses were hurt since black people could not get to the stores to shop. On November 13, 1956, the bus company finally agreed to end segregation, hire black drivers, and treat all riders with respect.

THE ROAD TO FREEDOM

That triumph in Alabama gave African Americans a new sense of pride! Folks in other cities followed and boycotted *their* bus companies. As all eyes in the nation looked to Montgomery, a new leader made his voice heard—a booming voice to which *everyone* had to listen. His name was Dr. Martin Luther King, Jr., and he would become one of the greatest leaders of all time.

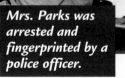

This telegram from a black church group to the governor of Florida threatened a boycott.

Imagine walking to school and being hit with raw eggs. Imagine being screamed at and called terrible names. How would you feel? That is what the first black students faced as they tried to attend white schools in the years after *Brown v. the Board of Education.* Segregation laws were crumbling, but there was still so much to do.

SIT DOWN, STAND UP

The late 1950s and 1960s were the years of the **Civil Rights Movement** and a time of **civil disobedience**— sit-ins, read-ins, and pray-ins. It was a time of marches and "Freedom Rides" on whites-only trains and buses. Blacks rose up to fight for their rights: The right to eat in *any* restaurant, to go to *any* school, to visit a library, to use a public restroom, or to vote.

In Greensboro, North Carolina, in 1960, four black college students sat down at a whites-only lunch counter. No one would serve them, so they sat until closing time. The next day they came back with more students. Soon hundreds of students, civil rights organizations, and members of the community joined in a six-month-long protest and boycott. News of the sit-in spread, and within a few weeks sit-ins were taking place in a hundred cities across America. Even being jailed would not stop them from making their voices heard.

DR. KING LEADS THE WAY

"In the end, we will remember not the words of our enemies, but the silence of our friends."

MARTIN LUTHER KING, JR.

Words to know

▶ **Sit-in**–
Refusing to move from a doorway, seat, or building to disrupt things in order to bring about change.

▶ **Civil Disobedience**–
(dis-oh-<u>bee</u>-dee-unce)
The act of opposing something that you disagree with in a peaceful way.

Virginia students take part in a sit-in at a lunch counter.

In 1960 a brave six-year old named RUBY BRIDGES became the first black child to attend an all-white school in the South. For an entire year no one would go to class with her. Only one person would teach her. Ruby is a symbol of courage to this day. On college campuses the fight to integrate was worse. People died in the struggle.

The Birmingham News
LATE FINAL

MEREDITH ENROLLS AT OLE MISS UNDER BAYONETS; RIOTS RENEWED

Two killed; 112 arrested

Free at Last!

"A man can't ride your back unless it's bent." So said Georgia-born **MARTIN LUTHER KING, JR. (1929-1968)**. Dr. King was a brilliant man—a man of faith—who touched people's souls when he spoke. For thirteen hard years he led countless marches and gave thousands of speeches, traveling over six million miles. Dr. King was arrested almost 20 times. His house was bombed. He was beaten and threatened with death, but he never behaved in an angry way, and he never gave up fighting for the rights of his people. As a Christian minister, he gave many inspiring sermons. Outside of church, Dr. King's powerful voice made black people believe that equality was possible.

1963 marked the 100th anniversary of the Emancipation Proclamation. In April of 1963, Dr. King led a huge march on Birmingham, Alabama, a city known for its terrible treatment of blacks. He knew America was heading toward trouble, but he was determined not to back down.

Dr. King was jailed during the Birmingham march. With a smuggled pen, he wrote a long letter from his cell on scraps of paper. The letter became world famous. Here is a part...

LETTER FROM A BIRMINGHAM JAIL

...[W]hen you suddenly find...your speech stammering as you seek to explain to your six-year-old daughter why she can't go to the public amusement park that has just been advertised on television, and see tears welling up in her eyes when she is told that Funtown is closed to colored children, and see ominous clouds of inferiority beginning to form in her little mental sky, and see her beginning to distort her personality by developing an unconscious bitterness toward white people; when you have to concoct an answer for a five-year-old son who is asking, "Daddy, why do white people treat colored people so mean?"...then you will understand why we find it difficult to wait.

Dr. King faced constant torment—arrests, beatings, death threats and jail, but his deep faith sheltered his spirit.

1954	1955	1957	1960	1961-62	1963
BROWN V. THE BOARD OF EDUCATION MAKES SCHOOL SEGREGATION ILLEGAL.	ROSA PARKS SPARKS MONTGOMERY BUS BOYCOTT.	NEW CIVIL RIGHTS ACT PASSES. U.S. TROOPS GO TO ARKANSAS SCHOOLS TO PROTECT BLACKS.	FIRST SIT-INS ARE STAGED. BLACKS HELP ELECT JOHN KENNEDY AS PRESIDENT.	FREEDOM RIDERS ARE ATTACKED. UNIVERSITY OF MISSISSIPPI IS DESEGREGATED.	DR. KING LEADS MARCHES IN SOUTHERN CITIES. WHITE VIOLENCE GETS WORSE.

The years between 1963 and 1970 were intense times. There were moments of great pride, but there were also moments of hatred, bloodshed, and death. In August of 1963, Dr. Martin Luther King, Jr. spoke on the steps of the Lincoln Memorial before a crowd of more than a quarter of a million people. To this day his words still echo in the hearts of good people who dream of a world where all are equals, but in the years that followed, violence would end his dream of peace.

SAD DAYS

A few months after Dr. King's speech, President John F. Kennedy was killed. A terrible sadness gripped the country. In the South, Ku Klux Klan attacks against African Americans became more frequent. It was a scary time. Many blacks felt unsafe.

How long can people be made fun of, bullied, and beaten before they cannot stand it anymore? Dr. King hoped to achieve change with peaceful methods, but other black leaders were sick and tired of waiting. They wanted action. They believed that if people got hurt or died, it was just part of the price of equality.

FROM HOPE

"...revolutions are never waged by singing 'We Shall Overcome.' Revolutions are based on bloodshed."

MALCOLM X

Dr. King at the Lincoln Memorial in Washington, D.C. on August 28, 1963.

Dr. King devoted his life to seeking change through peaceful ways. In 1964 he won the Nobel Peace Prize— one of the world's greatest honors.

"I HAVE A DREAM"

I have a dream that one day on the red hills of Georgia, the sons of former slaves and the sons of former slave owners will be able to sit down together at the table of brotherhood.

...I have a dream that my four little children will one day live in a nation where they will not be judged by the color of their skin but by the content of their character. I have a dream <u>today</u>!

AUG. 1963	1964	AUG. 1965	AUG. 1965	JULY 1967	APR. 1968
DR. KING DRAWS 250,000 PEOPLE TO WASHINGTON D.C. TO PROTEST SEGREGATION.	IN MISSISSIPPI "FREEDOM WORKERS" HELP BLACKS REGISTER TO VOTE.	VOTING RIGHTS ACT BECOMES LAW, OUTLAWING SPECIAL "TESTS" IN ORDER TO VOTE.	WATTS RIOTS ERUPT LEAVING 34 DEAD, 900 HURT, AND 4,000 ARRESTED.	ARMED FORCES ARE BROUGHT IN TO STOP RIOTS IN NEWARK, NEW JERSEY AND DETROIT, MICHIGAN.	DR. KING IS SHOT IN MEMPHIS, TENNESSEE. HIS DEATH SETS OFF MORE RIOTS.

TO TEARS

After a terrible childhood, Malcolm Little (1925-1965) ended up in jail. While there, he heard a man named ELIJAH MUHAMMED speak about the Islamic faith and became a Muslim. He changed his name to MALCOLM X, and when he got out of jail, he became a minister. At first he spoke angrily against whites, saying it was time for revolution, but in 1965, after a religious trip, he grew less **radical**. He was killed while giving a speech. Some believe he was shot because he had grown too "soft."

Words to know

▶ **Radical–**
(rad-ick-ul)
A new way of doing things, sometimes using force or violence.

FROM NON-VIOLENCE TO BLACK POWER

Unfair voting laws in the deep South made it almost impossible for a black person to vote. For example, more than 75 percent of blacks in Alabama could not vote because they had to pass special tests that asked ridiculous questions, such as, "At what time of day does the President stop being President when his term is over?"

How would you feel if you lived in a land where your voice was not heard, or where you could be thrown in jail for the smallest reason? Imagine being turned down for jobs so you could not feed your family, yet you still had to pay taxes and obey the laws. It was all too much! Peaceful means were not working quickly enough. Starting in 1965, many black communities exploded in anger and rage.

MAJOR MILESTONES
Sad Seasons

On September 15, 1963, just a few weeks after Dr. King's great speech, four young girls were killed by a Klan bomb tossed into a church in Birmingham, Alabama. The following summer three college students helping black people register to vote in Mississippi were killed by Klansmen, but no one was punished.

By the summer of 1965, some blacks were so frustrated that they started riots in Watts, a part of Los Angeles, California. More riots followed in the summers of 1966-1967. Things got so bad in Detroit, Michigan, and Newark, New Jersey, that the U.S. Army was called in to restore order. The saddest day of all came on April 4, 1968, when Dr. King was shot and killed after a speech to striking workers in Memphis, Tennessee. America wept.

59

BLACK POWER, BLACK PRIDE

"We'd rather die on our feet than be livin' on our knees. Say it loud, I'm black and I'm proud."

JAMES BROWN, BLUES SINGER

With fists raised in the black power salute, track stars *TOMMIE SMITH* and *JOHN CARLOS* received their gold medals at the 1968 Summer Olympic Games in Mexico City. Their proud salute, as the American flag was raised, caused a stir all across the world.

STOKELY CARMICHAEL (1941-1998) started a student group to help blacks register to vote—SNCC, the Student Non-violent Coordinating Committee. He went on to write a book calling for black power—and for people of African descent to grab control of their futures. In 1969 he moved to Guinea, in West Africa. He changed his name to KWAME TURE and worked for social change around the world.

Out of all the sadness of the 1960s, a powerful new feeling grew for many African Americans. Tired of trying to become a part of the white world, some people of color proudly said, "Black is beautiful."

POWER TO THE PEOPLE

Black students demanded classes on black history, and a college student named Stokely Carmichael called out for **black power**. Anger mixed with pride and led to the start of a group called the **Black Panthers**. The Panthers tried to help black communities. They served free breakfasts and started health-care programs, but wearing black berets and leather jackets with fists raised high, they could seem very scary. Their spokesperson, Eldridge Cleaver, said it best: "You're either part of the solution or you're part of the problem."

BOBBY SEALE and HUEY NEWTON were the leaders of the Black Panthers. Both ended up in jail, as did ANGELA DAVIS, a college professor and political activist. All three became world-famous.

60

NEW HEROES

Slowly but surely, black voices made themselves heard in America. People of color were elected to the U.S. Congress. African-American Studies departments appeared at many colleges. Big American cities elected black mayors. There were TV shows with black actors playing leading roles instead of maids or waiters. African Americans were now movie stars. Black doctors (who had pioneered open heart surgery in the late 1800s) continued to make medical miracles. Black athletes broke world records. There was even a brand-new holiday, **Kwanzaa** (which means first fruits in Swahili, an African language), started in 1966 by Ron Karenga, a professor in California, to celebrate African roots. The years of discrimination that had shut blacks out of the American dream were slowly beginning to fade, but there was still a lot to do.

BILL COSBY, SIDNEY POITIER, and DIAHANE CARROLL broke down color barriers on TV and in the movies.

MUSIC KEEPS THE PEACE
The Motown Sound

One thing seemed to unite people of every race—music. One of America's favorite sounds came out of Detroit, Michigan. Motown was short for "motor town" because all the major car makers had factories near Detroit.

BERRY GORDY was the genius behind Motown Records (read more on page 79). His idea was simple. Find great singers. Get great songs. Dress the singers in elegant costumes. Finally, add cool dance steps. It was a great formula. America fell in love with groups such as the Jackson Five, the Supremes, the Temptations, Smokey Robinson and the Miracles, and Little Stevie Wonder. In a time when black and white seemed so far apart, music brought us together.

DIANA ROSS AND THE SUPREMES made America stop and listen to "Stop in the Name of Love" and other top ten hits.

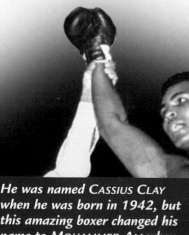

He was named CASSIUS CLAY when he was born in 1942, but this amazing boxer changed his name to MOHAMMED ALI when he joined the Muslim faith. He became the most famous athlete in the world—a man known as "the Greatest," and the "Sportsman of the Century."

"I Heard it Through the Grapevine" was a huge hit for THE TEMPTATIONS.

61

TAKING ACTION

"Our flag is red, white and blue, but our nation is a rainbow—red, yellow, brown, black and white—and we're all precious in God's sight."

REV. JESSE JACKSON

Words to know

▶ **Affirmative action–**
(uh-<u>firm</u>-uh-tiv · <u>ak</u>-shun)
A plan to make sure that job or school applicants are not treated unfairly because of race, class, sex, national origin, color, or religion.

▶ **Minority–**
(my-<u>nar</u>-uh-tee)
A part of a population that differs from the larger part in some way.

Who do you think will win this race? What would help the African-American child get to the finish line?

How do you correct a bad mistake? How do you undo the wrongs of hundreds of years? Even though laws had been passed to protect people of color from discrimination, it wasn't enough. In 1965 President Lyndon Johnson issued an executive order that said that businesses that received money from the government had to try to do even more to help **minority** groups. They had to take **affirmative action**.

FAIR OR UNFAIR?

For many, many years, white people—especially those with a lot of money—had advantages when it came to going to a good college or getting hired for jobs. How could a black person without a lot of money have the same chances?

All the hard work of the Civil Rights movement had led to change. Affirmative action pushed colleges to accept black students and to offer financial help. Companies began to run special training programs to help minority groups learn new skills. These programs gave people of color the chance to finally get ahead.

People who believe in affirmative action say these programs help make up for years of unfair treatment, but people who do not like the laws say that it all adds up to "reverse discrimination" against white people. Who do you think is right?

This girl is part of an affirmative action program to help minority students excel in science.

MAJOR MILESTONES
A New Kind of Rainbow

The Reverend JESSE JACKSON (1941-), learned a lot as he worked side by side with Martin Luther King, Jr. After Dr. King's death, Jackson started his own civil rights group and eventually decided to run for President of the United States. He formed a group called the **Rainbow Coalition**, which welcomed people of every race, color, and belief, and tried to win the Democratic nomination for President in 1984. Even though he did not win, his ideas for America made everyone take notice of him. Four years later he tried again and received even more votes! He still did not win, but Jackson became a force to be listened to and has kept on working to improve life for America's minorities.

TIME

THE JACKSON FACTOR
Black Pride, White Concerns

COLIN POWELL (1937-) began his career as a soldier and was wounded twice in combat. For his bravery he won two Purple Hearts, a Bronze Star, and many other medals, but that was only the beginning. He led the armed forces to victory in the Persian Gulf and by 1989 became Chairman of the Joint Chiefs of Staff—in charge of the entire military—the first black person to have that job. In 2000 Powell became the U.S. Secretary of State, one of the President's most important advisors. Dignified, smart, and honest, he has earned the respect of all Americans.

LEADING AMERICA

As police chiefs, city mayors, state governors, United States senators, generals and admirals, advisors to the President, and Supreme Court justices, African Americans have led with honor and courage. We look to all these great women and men and see that anything is possible with hard work.

Because of affirmative action, kids who might not have ever gone to college have graduated and become scientists, doctors, lawyers, and businessmen. With black people running cities, states, and the armed forces, discrimination will start to fade away. With a new generation of heroes to look up to, we can *all* believe that nothing is impossible.

*In **The Cosby Show** BILL COSBY played a doctor married to a lawyer. Cosby's gentle comedy became a hit while changing people's ideas about black families.*

63

WHAT COMES NEXT?

"When I look into the future, it's so bright it burns my eyes."

OPRAH WINFREY

Television shows like Grey's Anatomy and ER have brought America face to face with African-American doctors and story lines that have nothing to do with skin color.

Supermodel Alek Wek

When we look at the people on these pages, we see talent, beauty, power, and grace—wonderful, exciting people who help make life better.

WHEN COLOR NO LONGER MATTERS

The lines that divided America into black and white are slowly being erased. Our nation is no longer black and white. Instead we have become multi-hued. People of color lead our nation, make our laws, protect us from harm, teach us, and save our lives. Folks of *all* colors groove to black music. We root for African-American athletes to bring home Olympic Gold medals or win the World Series. We go to movies starring black actors.

It has been almost 400 years since the first Africans came to America—400 years of sadness, struggle, and sorrow. But all that is changing now, as African Americans step up to lead and help to shape the future.

WHAT AMERICA LISTENS TO
Hip-Hop Nation

Rap and **hip-hop** are two of the hottest sounds around, and their roots go way back, all the way to Africa's ancient kings and the singer/storytellers who sang of their leader's triumphs.

Rap music was born in New York in the 1970s. It was started by DJs playing records at parties who made up clever rhymes as they changed records. Soon "rapping" became a way to keep kids from joining gangs—a way to "fight" with words instead of fists. Soon there were cool dance moves to go with the new sounds. Break-dancing, with its head-spinning and acrobatic moves, is the best known. Walk into any health club today and you just might see a group of grannies taking a hip-hop dance class!

"The Audacity of Hope"

...It's the hope of slaves sitting around a fire singing freedom songs...the hope of a skinny kid with a funny name who believes that America has a place for him too. Hope—hope in the face of difficulty. Hope in the face of uncertainty. The audacity of hope! In the end, that is God's greatest gift to us, the bedrock of this nation. A belief in things not seen. A belief that there are better days ahead.

—BARACK OBAMA

Meet golfer Tiger Woods on page 71

OUT OF AFRICA

Today people from Africa are coming to America because they *want* to—drawn by the promise of decent jobs, and the hope for a safer life for their families. So much has changed since 1600, but it has been a long, hard journey to get to where we are today.

A BRIGHTER FUTURE?

We can only hope that with each passing day, the lines that divide us because of skin color will blur even more. Perhaps one day in the not too distant future, color will not matter at all. But right now, even though African Americans have become role models and heroes, discrimination and racism still exist. It is up to each of us to see to it that it ends. Martin Luther King, Jr.'s famous dream is still a goal for many African Americans. The day when people "...will not be judged by the color of their skin but by the content of their character" is still America's great quest.

CHAPTER SIX–GREAT LIVES

PEOPLE WHO CHANGED OUR LIVES

“From what we get, we can make a living; what we give, however, makes a life.”

ARTHUR ASHE

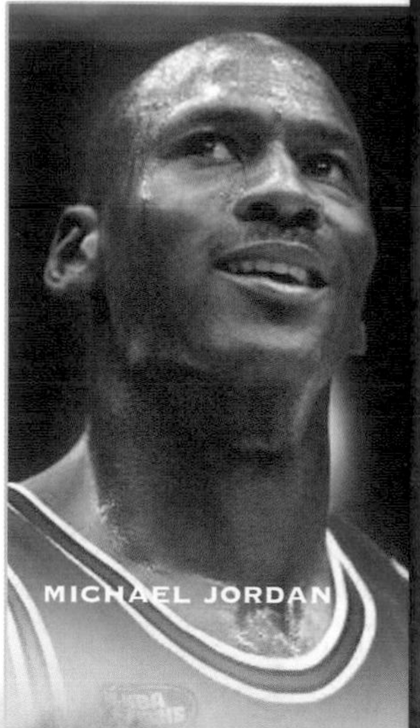

MICHAEL JORDAN

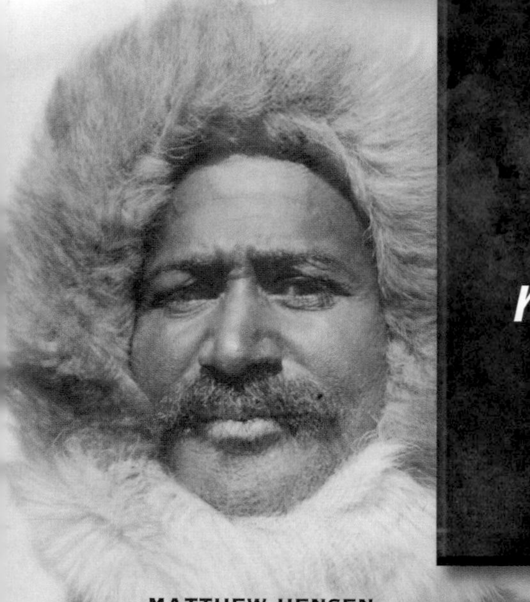

MATTHEW HENSEN

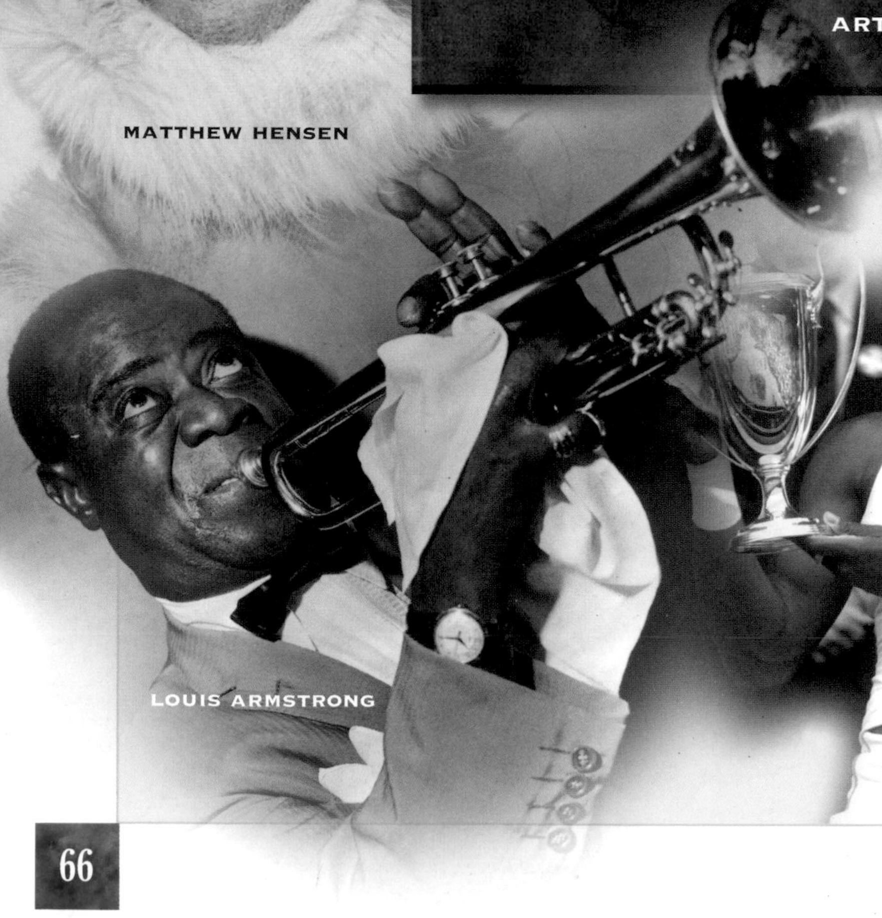

LOUIS ARMSTRONG

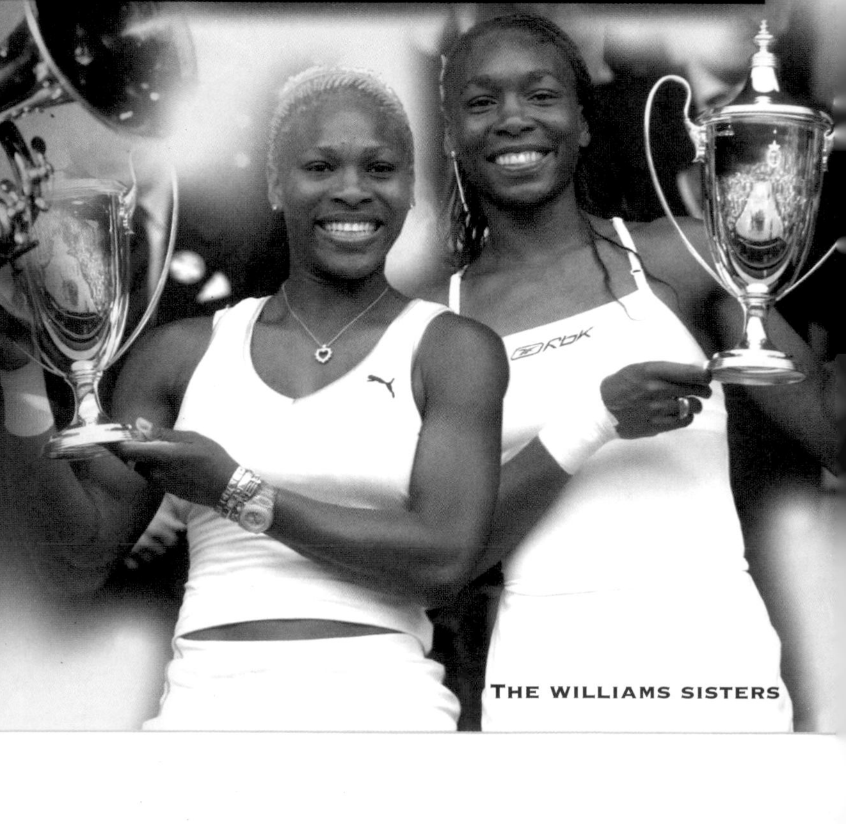

THE WILLIAMS SISTERS

Every life is important. Every woman, man, and child has the power to reach out, help others, and change things. Here are just a few of the people who studied harder, worked longer, tried more, and never gave up, even when their goals seemed impossible.

Some left their marks in science labs, discovering new ways to do things that made life safer, healthier, or easier. Some jumped higher or ran faster and along the way showed the world what the words "dignity" and "courage" mean. Some ventured off to explore the unknown. Others stayed closer to home to teach, to write, to make music, and to bring us joy.

AN INSPIRING JOURNEY

African Americans have changed the way America and the world work and play. The songs we sing, the books we read, the games we play, and the food we eat have all been shaped by a group of remarkable people. You have already met many amazing people. Now meet a few more...

MARY MCLEOD BETHUNE

GEORGE WASHINGTON CARVER

HALLE BARRY AND DENZEL WASHINGTON

CORETTA SCOTT KING

THURGOOD MARSHALL

AMAZING INVENTORS AND SCIENTISTS

"When you do the common things in life in an uncommon way, you will command the attention of the world."

GEORGE WASHINGTON CARVER

BENJAMIN BANNEKER
1731-1806

One of the brightest minds of his time, Banneker built the first working clock made entirely in America. He was also a gifted scientist, astronomer, writer, map-maker, and a brilliant city planner. He helped design the way the streets in the city of Washington, D.C. were laid out.

JAMES FORTEN 1766-1842

After serving in the Revolutionary War, Forten invented a way for sailors to pull huge sails up more easily. He ended up owning a successful sail-making company and used his wealth and standing in the community to fight for an end to slavery.

GARRETT MORGAN
1877-1963

Can you imagine driving in a busy town without any traffic signals? Morgan invented the first three-position traffic signal, which made city streets much safer. He also invented the first gas mask, and he made news when he rescued a group trapped by an explosion in a deep tunnel. A later version of his mask saved lives during World War I.

Benjamin Banneker

Black Heritage USA 15c

GEORGE WASHINGTON CARVER
ABOUT 1865-1943

Sickly as a child, young Carver spent a lot of time hanging around the gardens of the Missouri plantation on which he lived. He was fascinated by nature and was always asking questions. Folks began to call young George "the plant doctor" since he knew so much about how to use plants. Carver went on to study at Iowa State University and is most famous for finding over 320 uses for peanuts and 100 different things to do with sweet potatoes and soy beans—such as making medicines and cosmetics. Carver's greatest contributions came as a beloved teacher at Tuskegee Institute—an inspiration to his students and one of the greatest botanists ever.

LEWIS LATIMORE
1848-1928

Soon after this Civil War veteran returned from the war, he began working for Alexander Graham Bell and then Thomas Edison. Latimore made many contributions to the invention of the telephone while working with Bell and helped invent street lamps while working with Edison.

ELIJAH McCOY ABOUT 1843-1929

Trains were how America moved in the 1800s. McCoy, the son of slaves, studied engineering and figured out a way to keep train parts oiled without having to make costly stops along the way. His invention was so amazing that when railroaders went to order the part, they always asked for "the Real McCoy," since his parts were so much better than the copies made by his rivals.

CHARLES DREW
1904-1950

A person who loses too much blood will die. Dr. Charles Drew figured out a way to store blood plasma and then started blood banks. His work helped save millions of lives. Dr. Drew started the American Red Cross blood bank, but during World War II he was told to keep "white" blood separate from blood drawn from African Americans. To protest, he resigned.

MAE JEMISON
1956-

The first African-American woman in space always loved science as a kid. Jemison became a doctor and went to work for the Peace Corps before NASA picked her to go into space in 1992. These days Dr. Jemison is very busy devoting herself to teaching and improving medical care in Africa.

AWESOME ATHLETES

*"I can accept failure.
Everyone fails at something.
But I can't accept not trying."*

MICHAEL JORDAN

Meet some of the fastest, bravest, strongest athletes ever—people who changed the face of sports...

- The Negro Leagues–page 50
- Jackie Robinson–page 51
- Jesse Owens–page 51
- Mohammed Ali–page 61

...and *these* amazing superstars.

MICHAEL JORDAN
1963-

No one dunked, dribbled, or jumped like Mike—the greatest basketball player of all time. With six NBA titles and 14 "Most Valuable Player" awards, no wonder people of every color said, "I want to be like Mike!"

WILMA RUDOLPH
1940-1994

After falling ill with polio, a disease that destroys muscles, little Wilma could not walk, let alone run. But by the time she was 20, she had become "the fastest woman in the world" and had won three Olympic gold medals.

JOE LEWIS
1914-1981

They called Lewis the "Brown Bomber." He was the winner of 67 thrilling boxing matches. When he knocked out a famous German boxer in 1938 in the first round, he became a symbol of hope in the dark days of segregation.

DOMINQUE DAWES
1976-

This tiny dynamo took to the bars and balance beams of Olympic gymnastics not once, but in three different Olympics. In 1992 she became the first African American to win an individual event medal in gymnastics and opened the doors for other young black athletes to follow in her path.

JIM BROWN
1935-

Sports writers have called this football hero "Superman" and "football's greatest running back, *ever*." Big Jim played for nine years and led the NFL in rushing for eight of them. He left football at the top of his game and went on to become a film star and role model.

ARTHUR ASHE
1943-1993

The first African American to win at Wimbledon and the Australian and U.S. Opens. As a child in Virginia, Ashe was not allowed to play in many tennis tournaments because of his color. He used his fame to fight racial injustice.

VENUS & SERENA WILLIAMS
1980-   1981-

When these two tennis stars first burst onto the scene, with beaded hair and racquets swinging, they were unlike anything the tennis world had ever seen. They soon became two of the most famous athletes in the world and inspired inner-city kids to head to the courts.

TIGER WOODS
1975-

When Tiger's dad began teaching his son golf, it was a sport played almost entirely by rich white people. All that changed with the rise of golf's first black superstar. Tiger made it cool to tee off, and many think he may be the best golfer ever.

MUSIC LEGENDS

"The only thing better than singing is more singing."

ELLA FITZGERALD

Toes tapped, fingers snapped, and hands clapped to...

- Spirituals–page 48
- The Blues–page 48
- Jazz –page 49
- The Motown Sound–page 61
- Rap and Hip-Hop–page 64

...and *these* musical superstars.

THE ENTERTAINER
A RAG TIME TWO-STEP
BY SCOTT JOPLIN

SCOTT JOPLIN
1867-1917

In the years between 1900 and the start of the first World War, ragtime became America's hottest music and no one wrote or played it better than this talented piano player. People of all colors loved to dance to the boppy beats, and Joplin's "rags" were the most famous of all.

JELLY ROLL MORTON
ABOUT 1890-1941

Even as a baby in New Orleans, beating on pots and pans, Ferdinand LaMenthe had talent. He grew up, changed his name, and became the man who created a musical bridge from ragtime to the blues to jazz. He became one of the most famous jazz musicians around.

MARIAN ANDERSON
1897-1993

This world-famous singer had a voice so beautiful that it made people weep. She used her amazing talent to fight racism. In 1939 when Anderson, who had sung for royalty in Europe, was told she could not perform in a whites-only concert hall in Washington, her supporters got the government to allow her to sing on the steps of the Lincoln Memorial. One of those supporters was the President's wife! It was one of the most famous concerts ever as Anderson sang before 75,000 people, and millions more listened on radio.

BLACK HERITAGE
USA 37
Marian Anderson

72

RAY CHARLES
1930-2004

In spite of his blindness, Charles played many different styles of music but gave them all a unique new sound. Blues, country, gospel, and jazz all blended when his fingers hit the piano keys, and his raspy voice filled the air. He also wrote some of our best-loved songs, including *Georgia on my Mind*.

NAT "KING" COLE
1919-1965

Gentle and easy-going, Cole had a smooth, silky voice. He began as a jazz pianist and singer but switched to pop music and became a huge star. In 1956 Cole became the first African-American host of a network TV show but often felt the sting of racism as he performed in concert.

ARETHA FRANKLIN
1942-

"The Queen of Soul"—that is what everyone calls this powerful singer with a voice "like iron wrapped in velvet." Franklin, like many African-American singers, got her start singing gospel music in church. By the late 1960s she was a huge star and a symbol of black pride.

STEVIE WONDER
1950-

Blind since birth, Wonder never let his disability keep him from living life with joy. A star since the age of 12, he has been inspired by many different musical styles from pop to reggae to ancient African sounds, writing and performing some of the most popular and famous songs of our time.

WYNTON MARSALIS
1961-

This awesome trumpeter is one of today's jazz greats, but Marsalis is also a brilliant classical musician. In 1997 he became the first jazz musician to win the Pulitzer Prize in music—a very important award—for his epic jazz piece about slavery, *Blood on the Fields*.

THE POWER OF WORDS

> "If there is a book you really want to read but it hasn't been written yet, then you must write it."
>
> TONI MORRISON

ZORA NEALE HURSTON
1891-1960

Hurston was a lively woman with a writing style that made people feel like they were in the same room with her. She is best known for *Their Eyes Were Watching God*, but sadly by the 1940s publishers would not print her books because of what she had to say about race in America. Hurston was so broke she had to work as a maid.

LANGSTON HUGHES
1902-1967

While working as a busboy, Hughes tucked three of his poems beside the plate of a famous poet. That poet was so impressed that he arranged a college scholarship for Hughes. After graduation, Hughes traveled around the world, writing vivid poems about the struggles of life in the African-American community. *Read a Hughes poem on p. 47*

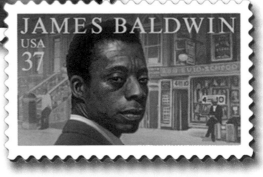

JAMES BALDWIN
1924-1987

Harlem-born, Baldwin was a leader of the Harlem Renaissance, but he moved to Paris—a place where blacks were accepted as equals. His most famous book, *Go Tell it on the Mountain*, is a story about an unloving father and his son—a tale that many felt was really about white America's treatment of blacks.

RICHARD WRIGHT
1908-1960

As a child in Mississippi, Wright fell in love with reading, but blacks were not allowed in public libraries. He borrowed a white man's library card and forged notes to the librarian in order to borrow books. His most famous novel is called *Native Son*—a book which showed that white racism would only lead to a terrible cycle of violence.

LORRAINE HANSBERRY
1930-1965

Her parents raised her to believe that being a black woman must never stop her from achieving her goals, so in 1959 Hansberry became the first black woman to have a play on Broadway. *A Raisin in the Sun*—the story of a family's struggle to survive—was a dramatic hit.

ALEX HALEY
1921-1992

After 20 years in the Coast Guard, Haley became a magazine writer. He interviewed many well-known people, but he is most famous for the book he wrote about his family's past. He spent 10 years researching *Roots,* which went on to win a Pulitzer Prize and become one of TV's most-watched shows ever.

TONI MORRISON
1931-

As one of the most famous African-American authors ever, Morrison's books have captured all the longing black Americans felt to be accepted into society. She is the first black woman to win the Nobel Prize in Literature, and she also won a Pulitzer Prize in fiction—two huge honors. She has been called one of the most important American authors of the 20th century.

ALICE WALKER
1944-

Her book *The Color Purple,* the very sad story of one woman's struggles to gain respect, won a Pulitzer Prize and was made into a powerful movie. Her biggest influence was Zora Neale Hurston, and she has helped bring Hurston's writing to a new generation.

MAYA ANGELOU
1928-

Angelou's life has been very eventful, with hard times as well as good times. She worked as a cook, a streetcar conductor, a dancer, and more. Then she took all her experiences and wrote amazing stories about them. Today, she is a world-famous writer and poet.

DANCERS & ARTISTS

> "...I have always worked just as hard when there were ten people in the house as when there were thousands."
>
> BILL "BOJANGLES" ROBINSON

HAROLD AND FAYARD NICHOLAS
1921-2000   1914-2006

Meet two of the greatest dancers ever to tap their feet! These brothers could spin, flip, and leap sky-high! Their parents were theater-folk, and the boys grew up in the company of performers. The amazing dancing duo became stars at Harlem's *Cotton Club.* By the 1940s they had tap-danced their way to Hollywood stardom.

BILL ROBINSON
1878-1949

Legend has it that this awesome dancer was named Luther at birth but hated his name so much that he forced his younger brother Bill to switch names with him! Nicknamed "Bojangles," this fantastic dancer could tap-dance up and down a flight of stairs. He still holds the record for running the 75 yard *backward* dash. He even danced for almost a mile down Broadway on his 61st birthday. He was a true legend.

KATHERINE DUNHAM
1909-2006

When she had to choose between her two passions, dance or anthropology (the study of humanity), she chose dance. Dunham became one of the world's most respected modern dancers and teachers, but she was also passionate about social issues. In 1991, when she was 82, she went on a 47-day hunger strike to protest America's overthrow of Haiti's president. The overthrown president had to come visit her to stop her from starving to death!

ALVIN AILEY
1931-1989

Ailey created dances that were unlike anything audiences had ever seen before—beautiful and powerful moves deeply rooted in African and Caribbean rythyms. His company had dancers of many colors and body types, which was a shocking thing in the 1960s. When Ailey died, he left the artistic direction of his company to his favorite performer, JUDITH JAMISON, one of the most talented dancers in the world.

AUGUSTA SAVAGE
1892-1962

Her dad, a minister, thought that making sculptures broke the Ten Commandments and forbade her to play with clay, but Ms. Savage loved art and became a sculptor anyway. She was turned away from art school because she was black, so she became an art teacher. Her mission was to give young African-American artists the chance she had been denied—the opportunity to study and discover the joy of being an artist.

Lift Every Voice and Sing

ROMARE BEARDEN
1911-1988

As a boy in Harlem, Beardon was surrounded by famous writers such as W.E.B DuBois, a friend of his parents, but Beardon loved drawing more than words. His style changed as he grew older, but his art was always bold and colorful—big paintings full of images of black traditions, religious themes, or simply the joy of musicians playing jazz late into the night.

JACOB LAWRENCE
1917-2000

Lawrence moved to Harlem when he was 13. His works were a celebration of being black in America. One of his first masterpieces was a 21-painting series about the overthrow of slavery in Haiti. Lawrence's aim was to give African Americans a sense of pride and hope at a time when racism made life very difficult.

ALL BUSINESS

MADAME C.J. WALKER
1867-1919

What would you do if your life was so hard that your hair started falling out? Sarah Breedlove found some creams that not only helped make her hair stronger and shinier, but she also started selling her hair potions to her neighbors and soon had a fine business. When she remarried, she began calling herself Madame C.J. Walker, hired a fleet of women to help her sell her products door-to-door, and became America's first female millionaire.

"...if I have accomplished anything in life, it is because I have been willing to work hard."

MADAME C.J. WALKER

MAGGIE LENA WALKER
1867-1934

The Virginia-born daughter of former slaves wanted to be a teacher but had to quit when she got married—the rule at that time. She got involved with a church charity, but when it ran out of funds, Walker had an idea. She asked folks to pool their money to be used for loans so that they could buy a house or send a child to college. Her idea grew into the St. Luke Penny Savings Bank, and she became the first female bank president in America. Her bank, now called the ***Consolidated Bank and Trust Company***, is still in business!

ALONZO HERNDON
1858-1927

Born into slavery, Herndon spent his free time as a child selling peanuts and homemade molasses to help his family. He saved as many pennies as he could, and when he had saved enough, he moved to Atlanta, Georgia, and opened a barbershop. Herndon turned that shop into Atlanta's finest, then took all the money he made from cutting hair and bought real estate. As his fortune grew, he started the ***Atlanta Life Insurance Company,*** and by the time he died, he was one of Atlanta's wealthiest men.

JOHN JOHNSON
1918-2005

In the 1940s there were lifestyle magazines for white people, but the only magazines for blacks were about civil rights.

Johnson borrowed $500 and in 1942 started *Ebony* and *Jet*. He filled the pages with stories about successful blacks, and in turn, Johnson became one of America's richest men.

ROBERT L. JOHNSON
1946-

What John Johnson did for magazines, Robert Johnson (no relation) did for TV with BET— *Black Entertainment Television*. He is also the first African American to own a commerical airline and a major league sports team.

BERRY GORDY, JR.
1929-

After years spent working on an automobile assembly line, Berry left to follow his dream—writing music. In 1959 he borrowed $800 to start a record company, and soon after, *Motown Records* was born. Gordy's ear and eye for talent helped him find many of America's biggest stars—artists such as Stevie Wonder and the Jackson Five.

RUSSELL SIMMONS
1957-

Rap and hip-hop are America's hottest sounds, and Simmons, the co-founder of *Def Jam Records*, is one of the reasons why. He was the first to produce rap records. Simmons also started *Phat Farm*, a company that sells rapper-style clothing. Simmons has used his fame and money to work for civil rights.

REGINALD F. LEWIS
1942-1993

Some kids dream of being sports stars or rock musicians. Lewis dreamed of running a big business. He studied to be a lawyer, then began buying companies that were not doing well. He helped each company run better, then sold each at a huge profit. He also gave away millions of dollars to charity because he knew that helping others was the best dream of all.

HIRAM R. REVELS
1827-1901

The nation's laws are made in the U.S. Senate and House of Representatives. That is where Revels, a preacher and teacher, served as the first black U.S. Senator in 1870-71. During Reconstruction—the years after the Civil War—there were many changes in U.S. law. Because of those changes Revels, a state senator in Mississippi, was sent to Washington. He served for over a year until the laws changed again and blacks swiftly lost all the gains they had made.

THE LAW-MAKERS

"If you're walking down the right path and you're willing to keep walking, eventually you'll make progress."
— BARACK OBAMA

THURGOOD MARSHALL
1908-1993

When Marshall was turned away from the University of Maryland law school because he was black, he vowed to use the U.S. court system to change the laws. He became a lawyer and played a huge part in winning *Brown v. the Board of Education*, which ended the days of separate schools for black and white children. His greatest triumph came in 1967, when Marshall became the first African-American U.S. Supreme Court Justice. For the next 24 years he was an important member of the highest court in our land, but he was saddened by the slow progress of civil rights.

JOSEPH H. RAINEY
1832-1887

In 1870 Rainey, who came from South Carolina, became the first African American to serve in the House of Representatives. The child of slaves, his dad earned enough money as a barber to buy his family out of slavery. Rainey followed in his father's footsteps and was a barber before getting involved in politics and running for political office. He was re-elected four times!

BLACK HERITAGE
USA
37
Thurgood Marshall

SHIRLEY CHISHOLM
1924-2005

When Chisholm, the first black woman to be elected to Congress, decided to run for President in 1972, some folks laughed. A woman! A black woman at that! But Chisholm was a fighter, and she made a serious bid for America's highest office. She also worked for equal rights for women at a time when they, too, faced discrimination.

CAROL MOSELEY-BRAUN
1947-

The first black female senator, Moseley-Braun, had two great passions—education and banning guns. After leaving the Senate she became the ambassador to New Zealand. Ambassadors represent their country in another part of the world.

L. DOUGLAS WILDER
1931-

Virginia-born Wilder was America's first African-American governor—the person in charge of running a state. After serving as governor, Wilder became the mayor of Richmond, Virginia, and is working to build the U.S. National Slavery Museum.

PATRICIA ROBERTS HARRIS
1924-1985

Harris had many firsts. She was the first black woman Cabinet member—part of a select group that advises the President. She held three different Cabinet positions. Harris was also the very first black woman ambassador and the first female to head a law school.

CONDOLEZZA RICE
1954-

The Secretary of State is the person who helps the President work with other countries around the world. It is a very big, hard, important job, especially when there are problems or wars going on among countries. Rice is the first African-American woman to have this job. Before that she was a college professor and also ran Stanford University, one of the nation's finest schools.

DOROTHY DANDRIDGE
1922-1965

Her mother moved to Hollywood to pursue an acting career, but beautiful young Dorothy was the one who ended up a movie star. She was constantly breaking down racial barriers. Sadly, in spite of her fame she had a very difficult life and died tragically.

"I sure am tired of drinking this colored tea"

HATTIE MCDANIEL

JAMES EARL JONES
1931-

The man with one of the most famous voices in the world had a terrible stutter as a child. He was so afraid to speak that he pretended he couldn't, but a wonderful high school teacher helped him overcome his fears. He has starred in over 150 films and many Broadway and TV shows.

BEST SUPPORTING ACTRESS
GONE WITH THE WIND
1940

Academy Award Winners

BEST ACTOR
LILIES OF THE FIELD
1963

BEST SUPPORTING ACTRESS
GHOST • 1991

HATTIE MCDANIEL
1895-1952

McDaniel was the first African American to win an Academy Award, playing Mammy, an iron-willed slave, in *Gone with the Wind*—a film about the end of the Civil War. But McDaniel was never invited to the movie's opening, and at the award ceremony she had to sit in the back of the room.

SIDNEY POITIER
1927-

Poitier came to America from the Bahamas and got his start on Broadway in *A Raisin in the Sun*. He was the first African-American man to win an Academy Award for his role in *Lilies of the Field*, playing a handyman working for a group of nuns. Poitier went on to become one of America's greatest stars.

WHOOPI GOLDBERG
1955-

This comedian/ actress wanted her stage name to be Whoopi Cushion to get people's attention, but her mom convinced her to use the last name Goldberg instead. She is one of very few people who has won an Academy Award, a Tony Award (for Broadway), an Emmy (for TV), and a Grammy Award (for music).

SCREEN

SPIKE LEE
1957-

There's a lot more to a movie than just movie stars. Lee is a person who directs movies. He has been the guiding force behind many great films about racial issues, especially the conflict between different ethnic groups when they must live alongside each other.

OSSIE DAVIS AND RUBY DEE
1917-2005   1924-

This husband and wife team were Broadway stars and film legends, but they are also known for their hard work for civil rights. They helped raise millions of dollars to fight racism and were friends with great leaders like Martin Luther King, Jr. and Malcolm X.

BEST ACTRESS
MONSTER'S BALL
2003

BEST ACTOR
TRAINING DAY
2003

BEST SUPPORTING ACTOR
MILLION DOLLAR BABY 2005

HALLE BERRY
1966-

Berry was raised by her mom in Cleveland, Ohio, and was named for Halle's Department Store—a Cleveland landmark. She is one of the most beautiful women in the movies and the first African-American woman to win a Best Actress Academy Award for her role as a struggling young woman.

DENZEL WASHINGTON
1954-

As a boy his parents would not let him watch movies, so it is amazing that Washington ended up as an actor. He plays good guys and bad guys with equal skill and is one of America's most famous actors. He was nominated for Acadamy Awards five times and has won twice.

MORGAN FREEMAN
1937-

Starring in a school play at age eight was the start of Freeman's love of acting. With money short he often collected soda cans from the trash to save enough to go to the movies. He is known for playing roles with great personal dignity. He won his Acadamy Award for his role as a weary boxing coach.

JAMES ARMISTEAD LAFAYETTE
1748-1830

Enslaved in Virginia, his master let Armistead volunteer to help the colonists during the American Revolution. Armistead spied for the Americans by "working" for British soldiers who never suspected a thing. He chose his new last name to honor the Marquis de Lafayette, a French general who helped the Americans win the war and asked that Armistead be set free.

HEROES & LEGENDS

"What was the point of being scared? The only thing they could do to me was kill me, and it seemed like they'd been trying to do that a little bit at a time ever since I could remember."

FANNIE LOU HAMER

ROBERT SMALLS
1839-1915

An experienced seaman, Smalls was the pilot of a Confederate steamboat. In 1862, while the white crew was ashore, he drove the ship across Union lines and told them where the Confederate Army was hiding. He became a Union war hero and went on to become a congressman for South Carolina after the war.

MATTHEW HENSON
1866-1955

At the age of 12, Henson saw an ad for a ship looking for men. He left home, signed up, set sail, and quickly learned to captain a ship. He lived in Canada with the Inuit peoples for a while and learned their ways before meeting Robert Peary. The two decided to explore the Arctic to the North Pole. Without Henson's help, Peary would not have made it, yet it took years for Henson to get credit for his work.

VIVIEN THOMAS
1910-1985

Thomas had saved money for medical school, but his dream was dashed when his bank went broke and closed. He got a job at a research hospital in Tennessee in the 1930s, kept learning on his own, and became a gifted scientist. He began working closely with a white doctor and invented a new way to save babies born with heart defects. Soon Thomas knew more than the doctor! He designed a special heart-surgery tool and often stood behind the surgeon in the operating room, offering guidance. It took 50 years for Thomas to get the recognition he deserved.

MARY MCLEOD BETHUNE
1875-1955

Teachers change lives, and Bethune, one of America's great educators, changed thousands. She started a school for black women with $1.50 in her pocket—raising money with pie sales and other fundraisers. In 1935 she formed *the National Council of Negro Women.* Her friendship with Eleanor Roosevelt, wife of President Franklin Roosevelt, led to better opportunities for African Americans.

CORETTA SCOTT KING
1927-2006

It is said that behind every great man stands a great woman. This is definitely true of Martin Luther King, Jr. After his assassination, Mrs. King picked up where her husband left off— working tirelessly for civil rights *and* human rights as she traveled all over the globe. She said, "Hate is too great a burden to bear. It injures the hater more than it injures the hated."

FANNIE LOU HAMER
1917-1977

Growing up poor in Mississippi, Hamer was so eager to learn that she picked up scraps of paper on the road so she could practice reading. In 1962 Hamer went to a voter-registration meeting and vowed to make sure black voices were heard at the voting booth. For the next 15 years she fought to give black voters a say in the political process. Sadly, she was beaten and sent to jail for her efforts.

HENRY "BOX" BROWN
1816-DATE OF DEATH UNKNOWN

When Brown's wife and children were sold to another plantation, Brown vowed to escape. He had himself packed into a crate and sent to the home of a member of the Underground Railroad in Pennsylvania. After word got out about his 27 hours in the U.S. mail system, Brown became very famous. He went on to write a book about his life and the evils of slavery.

MAMIE "PEANUT" JOHNSON
1935-

A woman playing baseball on a professional men's team? Impossible? When she was 17, Johnson hoped to play in the white women's baseball league but was turned away because of her color. She decided to try out for a men's Negro League team and made it! She was a great pitcher, but because she was so tiny, folks started calling her "peanut." In three years pitching she had 33 wins and only eight loses.

INSPIRING LIVES

"Buoyed up by the propect of freedom...I was willing to dare even death itself."

HENRY "BOX" BROWN

BUCK O'NEIL
1911-2006

Like Jackie Robinson, O'Neil also broke barriers. In 1962 he became the first African-American major league baseball coach, but often said that he treasured his days in the Negro Leagues because the quality of the game was so amazing.

MARY "STAGECOACH" FIELDS
1832-1914

Six feet tall, tough and strong, this fearless ex-slave moved to Montana at the age of 52 and began to drive a U.S. Mail coach. She never missed one day's work in spite of blizzards, hail, or heat and earned her nickname because she was always on time. She was a legend in the West.

Parks holds up one of his favorite photographs.

GORDON PARKS
1912-2006

Parks was a homeless orphan by the time he was 16, but a copy of LIFE magazine and an old camera changed his life. Parks grew up to become one of the world's most famous photographers. He took pictures of everything from high fashion to the horrors of war and went on to direct movies, write books, and compose music. His life's mission was to "...use my camera to speak for people who are unable to speak for themselves."

KEVIN CLASH
1960-

People are always surprised to learn that "Elmo," *Sesame Street's* furry red monster, is a "brother." As a kid growing up with sports-crazy friends, Clash was always teased because he loved puppets, but his passion helped him win millions of fans—young and old.

MARY FRANCIS BERRY
1938-

The fight for civil rights still goes on, and Dr. Berry, a brilliant educator, is a leader in that fight. President Carter named her a Commissioner on the U.S. Commission on Civil Rights. After the next President, Ronald Reagan, fired her for criticizing him, she sued him and won her job back. She became known as the person the President could not fire. In 1993 President Clinton named her Chairperson of the Civil Rights Commission. She also started a group to fight **apartheid**—the terrible treatment of blacks in South Africa.

LONNIE JOHNSON
1949-

This fun loving inventor was a rocket scientist at NASA. He came up with the idea for a high-powered water gun while experimenting in his bathroom with pumps. Since then almost 50 million *Super Soakers*® have been sold!

LAWS & PROCLAMATIONS

The Declaration of Independence

"...I do order and declare that all persons held as slaves within said designated States, and parts of States, are, and henceforward shall be free..."

ABRAHAM LINCOLN, EMANCIPATION PROCLAMATION • 1863

A draft of the Emancipation Proclamation, handwritten by Abraham Lincoln.

One of the ways things change is with the passing of new laws. Over the years many laws were written to deal with the buying, owning, and selling of slaves. Emancipation brought more laws that were often changed. Some laws were horrible and unfair—written to take rights away. Others were good laws that were supposed to protect the rights of African Americans. Unfortunately, some people worked against the good laws. To make things even more complicated, there were different national laws that covered the entire country, and state and city laws that applied to smaller areas. Here are a few of those laws.

| − STATE OR LOCAL LAW THAT TOOK AWAY RIGHTS | − NATIONAL LAW THAT TOOK AWAY RIGHTS | + STATE OR LOCAL LAW THAT ADDED RIGHTS | + NATIONAL LAW THAT ADDED RIGHTS |

⊖ 1641: MASSACHUSETTS
Slavery is declared legal.

⊖ 1662: VIRGINIA
A child born to a woman who is a slave is also a slave. A child born to a free woman is free.

⊖ 1663: VIRGINIA
All blacks, even those who were free, are now slaves. All newborn black children are now slaves even if their mothers were free.

⊖ 1705: MASSACHUSETTS
Marriage between blacks and whites is forbidden by law.

⊖ 1705: VIRGINIA SLAVE CODES
These laws take away all rights of slaves.

⊖ 1740: SOUTH CAROLINA
The Negro Act makes it illegal for slaves to gather in groups, earn money, learn to read, or raise food. Owners can kill rebellious slaves.

⊕ 1776: DECLARATION OF INDEPENDENCE
"All men are created equal," it says, but the man who wrote it, Thomas Jefferson, was a slave owner, and the freedoms hoped for in the Declaration were not meant to include slaves.

⊕ 1777: VERMONT
Slavery is abolished.

✚ 1783: MASSACHUSETTS

Slavery is banned. Black men can vote.

⊖ 1788: U.S. CONSTITUTION

The "three-fifths clause" declares that slaves will be counted as three-fifths of a white person for representation in Congress.

⊖ 1793: NATIONAL LAW

The first Fugitive Slave Law allows slave owners to pursue fugitive slaves across state lines. It is against the law to help fugitive slaves.

✚ 1794: NATIONAL LAW

Congress prohibits the slave trade between the U.S. and other countries.

⊖ 1806: VIRGINIA

A law is passed that makes it necessary for freed slaves to leave the state within one year.

⊖ 1819: VIRGINIA

Blacks are prohibited from learning to read and write.

⊖ 1820: CHARLESTON, SOUTH CAROLINA

Slaves are required to wear distinctive I.D. tags. This law is later extended to free blacks in the city as well.

✚⊖ 1820: MISSOURI COMPROMISE

Slavery is declared illegal in the territory north of the Missouri border. Missouri is admitted as a slave state, and Maine is admitted as a free state.

✚ 1826: PENNSYLVANIA

Anti-kidnapping laws protect free blacks.

⊖ 1836: TEXAS

Texas wins independence from Mexico and legalizes slavery. Free blacks and mixed-race people are forbidden to enter the state.

⊖ 1857: SUPREME COURT RULE

The **Dred Scott Decision** denies citizenship to all slaves, ex-slaves, and slave descendants, even those who move to a free state.

⊖ 1859: ARIZONA

Arizona declares that all free blacks in the territory will be considered slaves on the first day of the new year. One year later (1860), Arizona issues an expulsion act that forces all blacks from the territory.

✚ 1863: EMANCIPATION PROCLAMATION

Abraham Lincoln declares that all slaves in the states that have left the Union are now free. (Slaves in the North remain enslaved.)

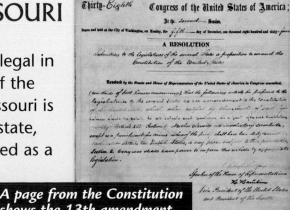

A page from the Constitution shows the 13th amendment, signed by Abraham Lincoln.

✚ 1865: 13TH AMENDMENT

This addition to the Constitution says, "Neither slavery nor involuntary servitude, except as punishment for a crime, shall exist in America." Slavery is ended in America.

⊕ 1866: CIVIL RIGHTS BILL

Gives blacks the rights of full citizenship: the right to own property, enforce contracts, and give evidence in courts—rights not specifically guaranteed in the Thirteenth Amendment.

⊖ The former Confederate States enact "Black Code" laws to counteract the thirteenth amendment.

⊕ 1867: RECONSTRUCTION

Congress says that Southern states will not be readmitted to the Union until they agree to the *14th Amendment*. With the exception of Tennessee, all the former Confederate states refuse to do so. They are divided into five military districts.

⊕ 1868: 14TH AMENDMENT

This addition to the Constitution says that all people born in the U.S. are citizens, no matter what their race.

⊕ 1870: 15TH AMENDMENT

Another addition to the Constitution says black males may now vote.

⊖ Some Southern states add "grandfather" clauses to their state Constitutions to block this ammendment. They write laws that say that the only people who can vote are those who had the right to vote before 1866 or 1867.

⊕ 1871: KU KLUX KLAN ACT

Gives the government power to punish violators of civil rights laws and was written to stop Klan violence.

⊕ 1875: CIVIL RIGHTS ACT

Gives blacks equal access to public accommodations such as trains.

⊖ 1877: COMPROMISE OF 1877

Allows for the withdrawal of federal troops from the South and the end of Reconstruction.

⊖ 1881: TENNESSEE

The first "Jim Crow" law is passed, segregating the state railroad. Other states soon follow and legalize segregation.

⊖ 1896: PLESSY v. FERGUSON

After Homer Plessy, who is only 1/8 black, is thrown out of a whites-only railcar in Louisiana, he sues the state. His case goes all the way to the Supreme Court where it is decided that separate facilities for whites and blacks do not go against the Constitution. This opens the door for all sorts of state laws that wipe out all the gains made by blacks during Reconstruction.

White people could go to the zoo in Memphis, Tennessee, six days a week. Blacks could only go on Tuesdays.

⊖ 1905: GEORGIA

This law requires separate public parks for blacks.

⊖ 1909: MOBILE, ALABAMA

This city law set a 10 p.m. curfew for blacks.

⊖ 1915: SOUTH CAROLINA

Blacks and whites are restricted from working together in the same rooms of textile factories.

The Brown girls had to walk through dangerous railyards to get to school. There was a whites-only school close by.

⊕ 1954: BROWN v. BOARD OF EDUCATION

The Supreme Court overturns the idea of "separate but equal," from 1896, ruling that segregation in public schools is no longer allowed.

⊕ 1961: EXECUTIVE ORDER 10925

Stops discrimination in federal government hiring on the basis of race, religion, or national origin.

⊕ 1964: CIVIL RIGHTS ACT

Ends discrimination by large private employers on the basis of race and gender whether they have government contracts or not. The Equal Employment Opportunity Commission is created.

⊕ 1965: VOTING RIGHTS ACT

Makes literacy tests illegal. Before this, some states made people of color take literacy tests with questions that nobody could answer in order to make it impossible for blacks to vote.

⊕ 1968: CIVIL RIGHTS ACT

Makes it illegal to discriminate in the sale, rental, or financing of housing.

⊕ 1978: UNIVERSITY OF CALIFORNIA v. BAKKE

Sets the standard of educational affirmative action. This law says that minority status can be used to decide admissions to colleges.

⊕ 2003: GRATZ v. BOLLINGER

The Supreme Court says that affirmative action must continue. Public universities may continue to use affirmative action to ensure a diverse student body.

The United States Supreme Court and the Capitol building (where laws are written) are two of the most important places Washington, D.C.

CHARTS & GRAPHS

WHERE ENSLAVED AFRICANS WERE TAKEN: 1492-1870

Most captured Africans went to Brazil. Others were brought to the small islands of the Caribbean to work growing sugar cane. After Portugal, which two countries brought the largest number of slaves to the Americas?

PORTUGUESE BRAZIL		4,000,000
SPANISH CARIBBEAN/CENTRAL AMERICA	2,500,000	
BRITISH CARIBBEAN	2,000,000	
FRENCH CARIBBEAN	1,600,000	
DUTCH CARIBBEAN	500,000	
BRITISH NORTH AMERICA	500,000	
DANISH CARIBBEAN	28,000	

0   500,000   1 million   1.5 million   2 million   2.5 million   3 million   3.5 million   4 million

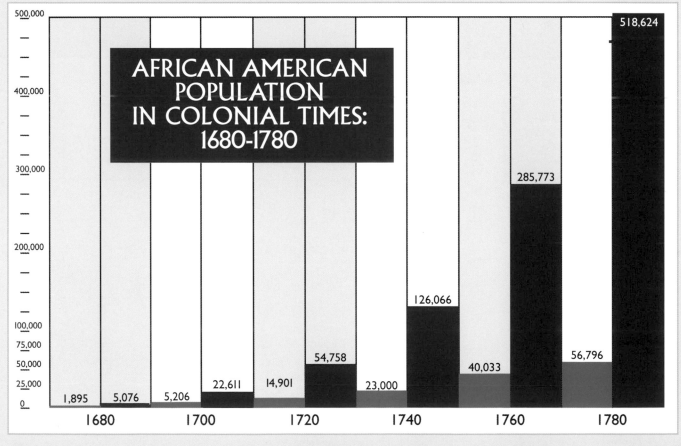

AFRICAN AMERICAN POPULATION IN COLONIAL TIMES: 1680-1780

Year	North	South
1680	1,895	5,076
1700	5,206	22,611
1720	14,901	54,758
1740	23,000	126,066
1760	40,033	285,773
1780	56,796	518,624

After the American Revolution black populations in the South grew quickly.

North   South

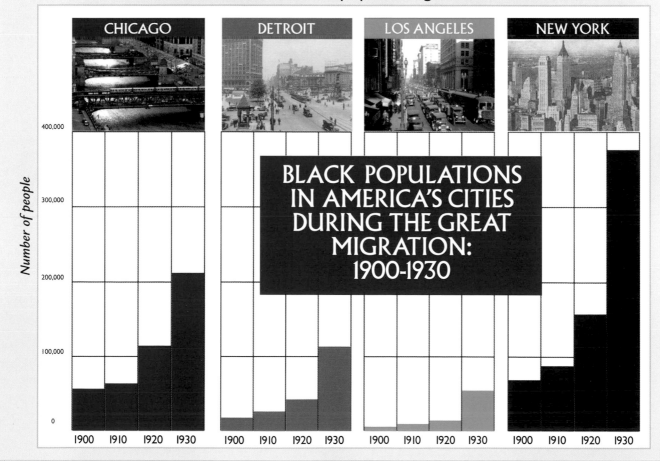

41.1　58.9

SOUTH CAROLINA

46.4　53.6

MISSISSIPPI

49.9　50.1

LOUISIANA

PERCENTAGE OF AFRICAN AMERICANS IN SOUTHERN STATES: 1873

During Reconstruction, the period that followed the Civil War, three states had more African Americans than white citizens. How do you think this might have changed the way black people were treated in these places?

By 1900, millions of blacks left the South and headed west and north to America's biggest cities. During this Great Migration, which city's African-American population grew the most?

CHICAGO　　DETROIT　　LOS ANGELES　　NEW YORK

BLACK POPULATIONS IN AMERICA'S CITIES DURING THE GREAT MIGRATION: 1900-1930

Number of people

400,000

300,000

200,000

100,000

0

1900 1910 1920 1930　1900 1910 1920 1930　1900 1910 1920 1930　1900 1910 1920 1930

RESOURCES FOR TEACHERS

• *In Motion: The African-American Migration Experience*

An in-depth online site supported with art and photography from the Schomburg Collection of the New York Public Library
http://www.inmotionaame.org/home.cfm

• *More famous African Americans*

An extremely comprehensive list of award-winning biographies, many of which celebrate unsung heroes or lesser-known African Americans. The list features reviews and suggested reading levels.
http://www.childrenslit.com/th_af_famous.html

• *African-American photo archive*

This University of Virginia site has a vast visual images collection of artwork relating to slavery.
http://hitchcock.itc.virginia.edu/Slavery/search.html

DISCUSSION POINTS

• Citizenship means having certain rights. Was it fair for black soldiers to fight in foreign wars such as 1898's Spanish American War, or World War I and II, without having the rights of citizenship in their own country?

• Race and the amount of money a person had were both important issues during the Summer of Red in 1919. At the same time as the riots were taking place, white working-class radicals were trying to push for a different type of government—one where there was no private property and goods were shared equally with all citizens. Do you think the radical workers and African Americans got along? What did they have in common? How were they different?

• Imagine someone has taken over your school and has made new laws that say you can no longer have recess. What are some ways you might go about changing the laws of your school?

RECOMMENDED BY LIBRARIANS

GRADES 2-4

Frederick Douglass: Portrait of a Freedom Fighter, by Sheila Keenan; Scholastic Books. An inspiring tale about a legendary civil rights leader.

Freedom Summer, by Deborah Wiles; Atheneum Books. Set in Mississippi during the summer of 1964, this is a lovely tale of friendship set against a backdrop of hate.

Grandaddy's Gift, by Margaree King Mitchell; Troll Communications. Determination in the face of prejudice in the struggle to vote.

The Hired Hand, by Robert D. San Souci; Dial Books for Young Readers. Based on an African American folktale.

Minty: A Story of Young Harriet Tubman, by Alan Schroeder/Jerry Pinkney; Penguin Books. Winner of the Coretta Scott King Award.

Sister Anne's Hands, by Marybeth Lorbieki; Dial Books for Young Readers. Set in the South at the height of the Civil Rights struggle, a white second grader finds herself in a class taught by a black teacher.

The Story of Ruby Bridges, by Robert Coles; Scholastic Books. Based on the true experiences of the first black child to attend an all-white school.

Sweet Clara and the Freedom Quilt, by Deborah Hopkinson; Dragonfly Books. A story of the Underground Railroad.

Uncle Jed's Barbershop, by Margeree King Mitchell; Scholastic Books. Surviving in the South during the Jim Crow years.

Wilma Unlimited, by Kathleen Krull; Harcourt Brace and Company. An inspiring tale about Wilma Rudolf.

GRADES 4 AND UP

Pink and Say, by Patricia Polacco; Philomel Books. A touching tale of two Civil War soldiers, one black, one white.

Roll of Thunder, Hear My Cry, by Mildred Taylor; Puffin Books. For ages 9 and up, a tale of courage in the face of the discrimination, set in the 1930s. A Newbery Award winner.

A Strong Right Arm, by Michelle Y. Green; Dial Press. An award-winning biography of Mamie "Peanut" Johnson.

SELECTED BIBLIOGRAPHY

• Appiah, Kwame Anthony, and Gates, Henry Louis, Jr., Eds. *Africana: The Encyclopedia of the African and African American Experience.* New York: Basic Books, 1999.

• Curtin, Philip D. *The Atlantic Slave Trade: A Census.* Madison: The University of Wisconsin Press, 1969

• Franklin, John Hope. *Mirror to America.* New York: Farrar, Straus and Giroux, reprint edition, 2006

• Hine, Darlene Clark, Hine, William C., and Harrold, Stanley. *African Americans: A Concise History (Combined Volume).* Upper Saddle River: Pearson/Prentice Hall, 2006

• Horton, James Oliver. *Slavery and the Making of America.* New York: Oxford University Press. 2005

• Katz, William Loren. *Black Indians: A Hidden Heritage.* New York: Aladdin Books, 1997

• McKissick, Patricia and Frederick. *The Royal Kingdoms of Ghana, Mali, and Songhay: Life in Medieval Africa.* New York: Henry Holt and Co., 1993

• Patrick, Diane. *The New York Public Library Amazing African American History: A Book of Answers for Kids.* New York: John Wiley & Sons, 1998

• Trotter, Joe William Jr. *The African American Experience.* Boston: Houghton Mifflin, 2001

• Wright, Kai, ed. *The African-American Archive: The History of the Black Experience Through Documents.* New York: Black Dog & Leventhal Publishers, 2001

• Unchained Memories: Readings from the Slave Narratives (DVD). An HBO Documentary Film in association with the Library of Congress; HBO Video. New York, N.Y. 2003

PICTURE CREDITS

The Kente cloth bands that appear throughout the book are handwoven by artisans in the African nation of Ghana.

INDEX